Who Kil

MW00439622

*Is
MADLIE*

*Love
Dad*

By Clive P. Oscar SFO

Clive P. Oscar SFO

Copy # 9

Who Killed the Christ?
Copyright 2009
Clive P. Oscar SFO

ALL RIGHTS RESERVED

Unless otherwise indicated, all scripture quotations are taken from the Ignatius Catholic Study Bible, Revised Standard Version, second edition.

ISBN: 978-0-9840914-0-9

For information contact:
Clive P. Oscar SFO
CliBet Publishing
P.O. Box 24
Kingsville, Oh. 44048-0024

Printed in USA
By Morris Publishing
3212 East Highway 30
Kearney, NE 68847
800-650-7888

Dedicated to the
Most Sacred Heart of Jesus
And the
Immaculate Heart of Mary

Think often of the Sacred Heart of Jesus and the Immaculate Heart of Mary.

Early in the morning, a lamb is led by a rope into the Great Jewish Temple on Mount Moriah. It is without blemish, a pure lamb. It will be offered to God by a Priest on this chilly morning as it is ritually slaughtered and its blood sprinkled about in atonement for sin. It is the morning sacrifice.

Outside, passing by is another lamb without blemish, a pure lamb, the lamb of God. He is being led by ropes to the Roman compound to be condemned to death. Later in the day he too will be led to ritual slaughter on Mount Calvary where he will also die and his blood will be poured out in atonement for sin. He is the evening sacrifice. The ultimate sacrifice; the Messiah, the Christ and the world will never be the same again.

Preface

Over the years there have been many arguments and discussions with regard to who killed The Christ. Many of these arguments have caused bad feelings to arise between religions and ethnic peoples.

Some say that the Jews and the Jewish leaders of the time, namely the Sanhedrin which was the governing body over all religious and civil affairs of the nation, were responsible for the death of Christ; particularly the former High Priest Annas and his son in law the reigning High Priest Ciaphas.

Others blame Judas Iscariot, the wayward Apostle for delivering him into the hands of Jewish authorities.

Then there is the role played by King Herod Antipas who adjudged him to be no more than a fool because he would not work a miracle in his presence for him and his court. Did he die because Herod, who could have released him and did not, delivered him back to the Roman Governor instead of exercising his authority over his own subject.

What about the Roman Governor Pontius Pilate who also could have released him. Without his consent no one could have put Our Lord to death as the Romans held all rights to level the death penalty to themselves.

What about the Roman soldiers who are credited for actually carrying out the execution with great abuse and brutality. Should we blame them for the death of Christ.

Many say that we can't blame any one individual or any race of people but that we must all take responsibility in a collective manner for his death because of our individual and collective sinfulness.

Who is right? Who did it? Was it the Jews or the Romans as a nation or was it Annas, Ciaphas, Herod or Pontius Pilate acting on their own. Are you responsible? Am I? Did we all have something to do with it? Who did it? Who Killed The Christ?

That is precisely what this book hopes to answer. To find out just who was responsible for putting an end to the most wonderful life ever lived. From the inception of the idea for this book it was determined that the best way to find out who killed The Christ was to try to find out just what happened on that fateful day in history when he was crucified.

To conduct a proper investigation one must always return to the scene of the crime but to conduct an investigation into a historical event is a little more difficult as we are far removed from the scene, the event and the time period. We must rely on historical writings, teachings and traditions. The saints and the Church Fathers as well as physical evidence such as relics and credible private revelations which have surfaced over the years are also great sources.

The first and most natural place to begin is Holy Scripture. The Gospels give a first hand account of what happened but unfortunately, only a brief account. Even with that in mind, it was found that in preparing this work there were many things contained in these brief accounts that landed on the author's ears many times in the past without properly registering what the gospel writer was trying to convey. It is not good to read scripture and then draw our own conclusions from it as we need to study it in earnest to find out what the inspired writer was trying to make understood. Most of us are not qualified to do this and must seek the help of the church by consulting works put together by bona fide scripture scholars. It is not only wise; it is recommended.

We must delve not only into the gospel accounts but also the Old Testament by also using the proper resources. Much is told about that day and what would happen on that day hundreds of years before it took place, particularly in the writings of the Prophets and the Psalms. A scripture scholar once said to a group I was in to read the Old Testament with an eye to the effect that everything in it points to The Messiah and it will become more understandable. I find this to be true but it is still easy to misinterpret what we read; so a great deal of caution must be used in its interpretation. Only good source material approved by the Church was used in preparing this work.

The early church fathers are a wealth of information. Many of them lived in a time when crucifixion was still in use. They were quite close to the story as they may have known people who where there or had access to the Apostles or Disciples. Some of them were themselves Disciples of the Apostles. They also had access to Roman records, writings and traditional stories. After all, a Roman Governor and a Roman Legion played a large role in the events of that day and the Romans kept good records. They also had access to the great libraries of the day such as the one at Alexandria in Egypt.

There are many relics in the possession of the church which are authenticated and speak to the events of that day. Many of them will be referred to in the footnotes throughout this book but I would like to touch for a minute on the shroud of Turin. It is probably the greatest relic in the possession of the church. I know that there are many who do not recognize it as the burial shroud of The Christ and I am not even going to get into that argument except to present the mathematical facts. In the time period before computers, all the facts known about the use of crucifixion, namely its six hundred year period of use , the number of people crucified as compared to the population of that period and all other pertinent facts and information were used to calculate the odds that the shroud of Turin was not the burial shroud of Christ. The odds were two hundred fifty five billion to one that it was not. In later years when the same information was fed to a computer to calculate, the odds were improved to one in ten billion removed to the tenth power. No investigator ever took evidence into court that was that convincing including DNA.

Private revelations were also used in preparing this work. I know that there are many who give no credence to private revelations as all public revelation ended with Christ. However, the greatest restraints were used in considering the contents of these revelations, namely; the Mystical City of God by Mary of Agreda, the Dolorous Passion of Christ by Anne Catherine Emmerich and the revelations of St Bridget. All these works are church approved writings. This does not imply that the church regards these writings in the same light as Sacred Scripture in that their contents must be believed but only that it finds nothing contrary to the faith which prohibits belief by the reader.

For the purpose of this work these revelations were treated as eye witness accounts in the following manner which I will explain. I know that many are not willing to treat visions, locutions, (interior voices) or apparitions as eye witness accounts. The reason they were treated as such for the preparation of this book is that over the years I have conducted many investigations and taken many cases into municipal, common pleas and federal court and have been a student of apparitions for more than thirty years. There is a great deal of similarity between the two in that mistakes can be made in both that are similar.

For instance a person may witness an event and not remember it exactly as they saw it. Certain details may catch their eye that another witness may miss. In the reverse, they may miss something that another person would catch. With all good intentions they may misinterpret what they saw or heard or may detract from it or embellish it depending on what they regard as important. There is always a possibility that they may misunderstand what is conveyed to them. None if this means that the event did not take place and that there is not a truth or message to be learned. It is in this respect that I treat them as eye witnesses.

Many have problems accepting visions, apparitions and locutions and dismiss them outright. In this day and age we have windows to the past in the form of movies, videos and CD's. A referee can watch a replay of an actual event and make a call on whether there was score or not. A video camera can catch a crime taking place and the results can be shown and viewed in a court of law. In documentaries we can see soldiers going ashore at Normandy or Iwo Jima. We regard these as credible but when God provides a seer with visions of the past we scoff and do not regard them as credible. Cannot God do anything we can do? Yes he can and he can also do it better. We can talk to people all around the world and even in outer space by way of a telephone; a voice inside a little electronic box. Cannot God communicate with whomever he wishes by using his own form of communication which is an interior voice? We can hide ourselves or show ourselves to other people whenever we wish. Cannot God do the same by way of apparitions? The answer is yes! That being said the only thing left to decide is whether or not what is revealed is credible.

What is revealed then, must be judged credible or not credible by proper authority. It must meet certain requirements. First, it must not take the place of, contradict, subtract from or add to Holy Scripture. Second, it must have been submitted to and interpreted by proper church authority and not by anyone else including the person to whom it was revealed. Third, it must not contradict itself. Fourth, it must make logical sense in the context of what is already known.

In preparing for this book I was amazed at how these different works written in different time periods and in different countries by people who never met or even knew each other complimented each other so well. The writing styles are very difficult to understand and must be studied, not just read. These writings were included in the overall research of this book because it is assumed that Our Lord, his Holy Mother and great saints have better things to do then going around the world dispensing useless information. There is a purpose in everything that God does and allows and none of it is useless or by accident. In private revelation there is something that God wishes us to know. As in all things pertaining to God he leaves it up to us to accept or reject. His holy church does the same.

You will notice throughout this work that there are many quotes. Those which are found in scripture and are well known are not footnoted. Those that may come from private revelation are quoted as to their source in the footnotes.

When I first set out to tell the story of the crucifixion I intended to tell it from a physical point of view only by documenting the arrest, trials, physical abuse and crucifixion. The more I dug into the research the more I realized that you can't separate the physical from the spiritual if you are going to understand what is taking place. This is a story of spiritual redemption brought about by horrible physical, mental and spiritual suffering by the God-man. We have to know what is taking place in both the physical and spiritual realm; the role of men; the role of Angels; the role of demons. For much is going on in the spiritual realm at the same time many things are taking place in the physical realm. We need to know what the Holy Angels are up to and why they do not, as it seems, interfere. We have to know what the demons are up to at different points in the story to know what drives men to do the things they do. We need to learn the whole story including the interaction of God the father with God the son and the Holy mother during all these events. In revealing the whole story we begin to see just how much God loves this creature he has placed on the earth and what kind of value he places on mankind.

So let us begin our journey into both worlds for they are very much interconnected. Lets us find out together, who killed the Christ?

The Author

Table of Contents

Chapter I
The Agony in the Garden

It was between eight and nine in the evening when Our Blessed Lord rose to leave the cenacle. The Passover meal was complete and he had celebrated the first mass. Leaving the upper room where all the festivities had taken place, he, along with his Apostles and Disciples made their way down the stairs to the ground floor level and began to leave the building when he met his Blessed Mother who had come from a separate room.

She fell at his feet adoring him as her true God and Redeemer. On the occasion of this meeting a deep sorrow which was beyond the understanding of Angels or men encompassed both mother and son. In his Divine majesty he looked upon his Mother with the tenderest love of a son and said to her; "My Mother, I will be with you in your tribulation. Let us [1] now accomplish the will of the Father and the salvation of men." She offered herself as a sacrifice and asked for his blessing which he immediately gave to her.

The owner of the building was present at this meeting between Mother and son and was deeply moved. Under Divine inspiration he put his entire household and all it contained at the service of the Holy Mother for the rest of her stay in Jerusalem. Our Blessed Lady humbly accepted his offer. The holy women of her company, who were many in number, stayed with her also. At all times, she was surrounded by one thousand Angels who made up her Heavenly guard.

Our Lord then left the building with his apostles and Disciples. Many of the Disciples left his company, going down different streets to attend to their own personal affairs. He is soon left with only his twelve Apostles.

---

[1] Notice that Our Lord said; "Let us, not let me." The role of The Blessed Virgin is little understood by most and will be dealt with throughout this work. There is a reason why the Church titled her "Coredemptrix. Quote is from the Mystical City of God by Mary of Agreda.

Dating by the Jewish calendar it is the fourteenth day of the month of nizan [2] which is the first month of the Jewish year. The evening is cool and bathed in soft moonlight for the moon is almost full. The peaceful glow of the moon renders a deceptive quality to a seemingly peaceful evening. There is no indication in the air that the most fierce battle ever fought between good and evil, life and death and light and darkness is about to get underway. The second Adam and Eve are on the verge of making right the shortfalls of the first Adam and Eve. The Blessed Virgin is already in position and Our Blessed Lord is on his way to the battlefield.

Our Lord and his Apostles turn southwest toward the Hinnom Valley and slowly walk down the long Old Roman steps toward the fountain gate which is located in the southwest corner of the walled city. They wander past the pool of Siloam [3] out the fountain gate and into the Hinnom Valley. Our Lord is leaving Jerusalem for the last time as a free man.

Once they were outside the wall, Judas decided that Our Lord intended to spend the night in the garden of Gethsemane [4] as he had done so many times in the past. This appeared to him to be a good time to deliver Our Lord to the Priests, Scribes and Pharisees in compliance with the deal he had made with them to deliver Our Lord for thirty pieces of silver. He had made this agreement while the other Apostles were eating the Passover meal. He began to purposely lag behind, letting the others slowly get ahead of him until he lost them from view. He then set off to the house of the High Priest.

Satan, seeing what Judas was up to and how he was determined to deliver Our Lord to his death decided to try to intervene. Even though he had goaded Judas into betraying his master, he was beginning to think that this Jesus could possibly be the true Messiah. He came toward Judas in the form of one of

---

[2] This corresponds to the 24th of March in our present day calendar.

[3] Our Lord had cured a blind man here by first putting mud on his eyes and then telling him to wash in the pool of Siloam.

[4] In Aramaic, Gat (press) Chemani (oil) Gethsemane means oil press. The holy oils used in the Temple are thought to have come from the olive groves in this garden.

his friends who already knew of his betrayal plans. In this form Satan could speak to Judas without being recognized for who he was. Satan tried to talk Judas out of going ahead with the betrayal telling him it seemed advisable at first but after more consideration he did not think it was advisable now. He advised him that Our Lord was not as bad as Judas imagined and did not deserve death. He also suggested to Judas that Our Lord might free himself by way of a miracle as he had done many times in the past and cause Judas great harm.

Filled with a new fear that Our Lord could be the Messiah, Satan tried to undo the suggestions with which he had filled the heart of Judas in the past when he wanted him to turn against his Master. [5]

Judas was not concerned with the arguments presented to him. He would rather take his Master's life then suffer the consequences of crossing the Pharisees. Judas paid no attention to the advice of Satan although he had no idea that he was not talking to his friend whose shape Satan had assumed. Judas had been stripped of grace and could not be persuaded to turn back from the completion of his evil plan.

As Our Lord and his eleven Apostles passed through the fountain gate they turned to the left and began to walk northward on a dusty road just outside the eastern wall of the city. This road was about six to eight feet above the brook Kidron [6] which was just off to their right. It flows through the Kidron Valley which is also known as the Valley of Josaphat. This valley runs north and south between the eastern wall of Jerusalem and the western slope of the Mount Olivet and is known to all the inhabitants of Israel as the valley of sin. In days past, it had been in this valley that sacrifices had been offered to the Pagan god Moloch. Each year the red cow is led out of the city over a specially constructed bridge over the brook Kidron and sacrificed on Mount Olivet and immolated in atonement for the people. In the same way, the scape goat is driven out once a year into the valley to be

---

[5] At this point Satan is unsure of just who he is dealing with in the person of Our Lord.

[6] Kidron means a dark obscure ravine, a vale of shadows.

devoured by wild animals to give satisfaction for sin in place of the sinners.

Now The Son of God is walking into the valley of sin on his way to offer himself up in satisfaction for sin. His soul is deeply oppressed and his sorrow is on the increase. He now plainly tells the Apostles all that will happen to him on this night and the following day. He tells them that they will be scandalized in him this night for it is written; "I will strike the shepherd and the sheep of the flock will be dispersed". But I shall rise again and go before you into Galilee. The Apostles crowded around him and expressed their love for him.

Our Lord continued to explain things to them in the same manner. Peter said to him; "Although all should be scandalized in you, I will never be scandalized." Our Lord replied to Peter; "Amen, I say to you that this night before the cock crows [7] you will deny me three times." Peter replied; "Even if I should die with you, I will not deny you." [8]

Reaching the bridge that spanned the brook they crossed over. One can only wonder at the thoughts of Our Lord as he crossed over the Kidron. This little brook ran directly past the eastern wall of the Temple. The plumbing for the sacrificial Altar was such that it collected the excess blood of animal sacrifice and discharged it into the Kidron. Our Lord was most assuredly aware as he passed over this brook that there were times when it ran red with the blood of sacrifice; a sacrifice which he was about to render forever obsolete with his own sacrifice.

Once they were on the other side they turned north again and wandered slowly along the Bethany road toward the garden of Gethsemane. They stopped now and then to converse and the Apostles could notice that the sadness of Our Lord continued to increase. They tried to comfort him by making all kinds of arguments that what he was talking about could not possibly

---

[7] Many writers refer to the third watch of the night which was known as the cock crow watch to be what Our Lord was referring to. Later on in the religious trials it will become apparent that he is referring to a rooster.

[8] Matthew, Luke and John place this objection of Peter in the Cenacle. Anne Catherine Emmerich and Mark put it on the way to Mount Olivet. Mark was Peter's Disciple after the Ascension.

happen to him. They finally grew tired of trying to argue the point and began to be assailed by doubts and temptations of their own.

As they neared the garden he told them that he would return one day to judge the world but not in a state of humility and poverty as he found himself now. He told them that men would tremble with fear and say to the mountains fall on us. At these words, the Apostles fell silent.

Our Lord's thoughts turned to his Most Holy Mother for he needed to find some object in creation in which his love could be returned and for a reason not to pay full attention to the dictates of Divine Justice alone. Only in her alone could he expect to see the full fruits of his passion and death. Only in her endless holiness could his justice find some return for the evil rendered by the human race. Only in her deep humility and constant charity could he deposit the treasure of his merits so that after his sacrifice his church might come into existence. The comfort which the humanity of Our Lord drew from the certainty of his Blessed Mother's holiness gave him strength and new courage to overcome the malice of mortals. He counted himself well repaid for all the suffering and pain he was about to endure because his Blessed Mother also belonged to mankind.

Having heard that Our Lord was in Jerusalem the Priests had come together to consult about the promised betrayal. This seemed to be a favorable night to effect his capture and they had already made great preparation, taking every precaution so that Our Lord would not be able to escape their clutches this time as he had so many times in the past.

Judas finally made his appearance and informed them that Our Lord and his other Apostles were now on their way to Mount Olivet to pass the night in the garden of Gethsemane. The Priests were overjoyed and began at once to assemble an armed force to make the arrest.

Our Blessed Lady, by way of a singular privilege granted to her by The Eternal Father and her Divine Son was able to witness from her retreat in the cenacle, all that took place in connection with her Most Holy Son. She understood the sinister thoughts of Judas. She watched him separate himself from the

Apostles, saw him in conversation with Satan and then help the Priests arrange for the capture of her Divine Son. Untold sorrow pierced her most pure heart and she wept bitterly over the loss of the faithless Apostle. She tried to make amends for his malice by adoring, confessing, praising and loving her most adorable Son. She offered herself to the Eternal Father to be allowed to die in her Son's place. She prayed earnestly for those who were now plotting his demise for she considered them as prizes to be valued according to the infinite value of her Divine Son's precious blood for which she foresaw they would be bought.

Our Lord and the Apostles had arrived at the foot of Mount Olivet and were standing on the Low Bethany Road which went north and then curved gradually to the east around the base of Olivet to the town of Bethany. Facing east, directly in front of them, the High Bethany Road went east up the mount for a short distance and then branched off to the left to go over the summit to the town of Bethany. It was known as a shortcut for those who could stand the rigors of climbing the mountain. At the spot on Mt Olivet where the High Bethany Road branched off, their stood an arbor and beneath the arbor another road branched off to the right and went southeast over the mount into the Jordan valley.

The garden of Gethsemane was divided into three parts. The largest part was located off to the right as one looked east up the mount. It was surrounded by a hedge and contained many fruit trees and flowers not to mention a few deserted sheds. To the left was a smaller section known as the Garden of Olives. It contained an olive grove and a press for making olive oil. This section was terraced and boasted many caverns. It was surrounded by an earthen wall. The third part of the garden was between the Low Bethany Road, on which they were standing and the brook Kidron. It was mostly unused and unkempt and contained a fairly large grotto. [9]

---

[9] Tradition holds that this garden was owned by the family of the Blessed Virgin and that the Apostles had the key to the garden. Her tomb was eventually placed in the wild part of the garden next to the grotto.

Our Lord began expressing deep sorrow and told his Apostles that danger was at hand. He told eight of the Apostles to stay in the larger part of the garden to the right of the arbor while he would go to another part to pray. He admonished them to watch and pray so that they would not yield to temptation.

He then took Peter, James and John and went into the Garden of Olives to the left of the Arbor. James and John, the sons of Zebedee were cousins of Our Lord but were endowed with better gifts then that of relationship. They had been with Peter on Mount Tabor when Our Lord had manifested his divinity and revealed to them that he was the fulfillment of the law and the prophets as witnessed by Moses and Elias. This night, along with Peter, they would be better able to endure the spectacle of their Master's great dejection than the eight who had been left behind.

Now the great hour of desolation is descending upon the soul of Our Lord. He is now upon the battlefield which he himself has chosen. It was in a garden; given by God to the first Adam and Eve that Satan had won his terrible victory. Our Lord, the second Adam is set to do battle in the Garden of Gethsemane owned by his Mother the second Eve. In a garden will his passion begin and in another garden will his body be laid when his passion has ended.

To his legions of Blessed Angels, Our Lord gives the signal that Satan and his cohorts have permission to approach and put forth their power against him as far as the decree of The Eternal Father will allow. Until he says the word and gives his permission, nothing can take place.

The demons need no encouragement. They are fully aware of the preparations against him, which are underway through their encouragement and prodding. What they do not know is that they are entering into an impossible conflict with their God. They believe that they are entering into a struggle against a just man, a prophet. No matter how holy he is, to them he is just a mere man and so they proceed daringly, boldly and hopeful that by exerting their energy and intellect they can cause his downfall. They do not know at this point that he is the Son of

God, the word made flesh as this is purposely withheld from them. So they proceed with reckless abandon.

In the company of his three Apostles, Our Lord raises his eyes to Heaven, to his Eternal Father and confesses and praises him. Internally he is praying for the fulfillment of the Prophet Zechariah [10] permitting death to approach and commanding the sword of justice to be unsheathed over him. He offered himself anew to The Eternal Father in satisfaction to Divine Justice for the redemption of the human race. He gave full consent for all the torments of his passion and death to be let loose over the portion of his being that was capable of suffering and asked that his suffering might reach the highest degree possible. The Eternal Father granted these petitions and approved his total sacrifice of his Sacred Humanity. Of his own accord, he made a beginning of his bitter passion by giving full liberty to the passions of fear, weariness and sorrow to come forth and afflict him. This prayer was the gate through which the multitude of his sufferings was to gain entry.

Immediately he began to plunge ever more deeply into sorrow and anguish of soul. Our Lord willed himself this anguish of soul to atone for mankind's abuse of the faculties of the soul through sinful thoughts, fantasies and sinful desires. He began to fear and be heavy of heart. He would begin his passion where the source of all sin begins, for from the heart and the soul come all evil thoughts, murders, adulteries, fornications, thefts, lies, blasphemies and all other sorts of vile sins. He was overwhelmed by sadness; sadness over our sins for which he wished to atone for all the pleasure felt by the sinner in satisfying their passions and lusts.

In the dim moonlight the Apostles witness how the pale of death has spread over his face and they become unsettled and horror stricken. His strength is apparently gone from his trembling body. Our Lord is now enduring, in its most aggravated form, all the anguish and distress which torments the

---

[10] The Lord Almighty says; "Wake up sword and attack the shepherd who works for me. Kill him and the sheep will be scattered." Zechariah Chap: 13, Vs 7.

dying when their greatest agony sets in and the soul mu. separate from the body. He is enduring all the bitterness of death without dying. If it had not been decreed from all eternity that he should die on the cross, he would have died here and now.

John said to him: "How is it that you who have always consoled us cannot now be consoled?" He replied; "My soul is sorrowful, even unto death. Remain here and watch with me. Pray that you may not enter into temptation."

His sorrow at this point is strong enough to break his heart and cause his death. He permitted his sorrow to reach the highest degree possible in his Sacred Humanity. This sorrow pierced the highest faculties of his body and soul by which he could see the perfect degrees of Divine Justice and the exclusion from salvation of so many for whom he was about to die. In order to deliver the world from sin and to no longer see his Eternal Father offended he had come upon the earth as God-Man to suffer a painful passion and death in atonement for sin, for as much as he loved his Father, was how much he hated sin and all the fruits of its malice of which he alone well knew.

His sorrow, rising from the natural repugnance to suffer and for the cruel death he was about to undergo was a minor fear to him. He did not say that he was sorrowful on account of his death but that he was sorrowful unto death. In the rest of us, fear of death comes from awareness of past sins, the uncertainty of what awaits our immortal soul and the natural reluctance of the soul to leave the body. Our Lord had no sins and he knew that he would go to The Father. But what he could see was that in spite of all his sufferings, there would still be so many sins committed in the world and his sorrow for this was far more than any sorrow that all contrite souls together could ever feel and was far more than every sorrow which could ever afflict a human heart. His sorrow was pure sorrow without any relief.

Extreme torment overwhelmed his soul and broken heart at the sight of all the sins of the world; all the blasphemies, sacrileges, impure acts and crimes to be committed after his bitter death. Each and every sin tore at his being with all the effects of its own malice. To perceive so much sin after so much suffering; so much sin after pouring out so much love; so much sin poured forth from the ingratitude of mankind makes him; "sorrowful unto death."

The immense love of Our Lord for us demanded that he suffer this mysterious sorrow to its absolute fullest. If he had let it stop short of the most sorrow that he was capable of suffering, his perfect love would not have been satisfied. He also wished it to be known that his love could not be extinguished by immense suffering and trials.

Even in the midst of all his suffering and sorrow, his concern for his Apostles brings his charity to the fore. He is genuinely concerned about them and does not tell them to pray not to be tempted but to pray that when temptation does come they might not listen to it and enter into it. Not once does he think of saving himself from anguish but he is anxious for his Apostles. He knows that they are greatly disturbed at seeing that his hour of suffering and death is unfolding before their eyes, even though he has tried to warn them of it many times. They are fearful and greatly confused without daring to speak of it. Our Lord tried to put them at ease by telling of his own sorrow unto death. By the sight of his own affliction and anxiety they were to take heart at the fears and anxieties of their own souls.

More than all the other Apostles these three had a better conception of the greatness and Divinity of Our Lord, as far as the excellence of his doctrine, the holiness of his works and the power of his miracles. They alone had been with him when he raised the daughter of Jarius and when he was transfigured on Mount Tabor, conversing with Moses and Elias. They understood more completely and wondered more deeply at his dominion over all creation. It was fitting that they should be in the garden to witness his purely human sorrowful affliction in order that they might be confirmed in their belief that he was truly a man capable of suffering. By the witness of these three Apostles the future Church would be able to refute for all time the denials of the humanity of Christ.

Our Lord now beheld suffering and temptations surrounding him on all sides, drawing near to him in the form of hideous figures. Leaving his Apostles by a large smooth rock [11] which protrudes about two feet above the ground in the Garden of Olives, Our Lord made his way down the slope of Olivet, climbed over the earthen wall, crossed over the Low Bethany Road and entered the wildest part of the garden between the Bethany road and the brook Kidron. He descended into a grotto about a stones throw from where the three Apostles were. Plants hanging down over the entrance to the grotto [12] conceal its interior.

It is now late evening, the time of the day when millions of people set out to seek the embrace of sinful pleasures. The God-Man descends into the grotto trembling and staggering as he tries to put one foot down in front of the other. The frightening figures surround him in an ever tightening circle. Once into the grotto he falls prostrate on the ground and prays. Our Lord is in a frame of mind where most of us would say we cannot pray. By praying while in such a torment, he shows by example that it is in such times that we need to pray. It is just such a time that the evil enemy attacks with temptations and if we are to resist in our weakened state, we must seek help. He prays while all but his enemies are sleeping. [13] He prayed while his enemies banded together to capture and kill him. [14]

He is crushed by the heaviness of fear, sorrow and sadness. He could at once rise up, throw off his feebleness and suffering and enjoy total happiness but with all his heart and soul he chooses to be here, to deliver himself up for the love of us. With complete compassion and total sympathy he enters into suffering with all who suffer.

---

[11] This rock is still to be found in the Garden of Gethsemane to the present day.
[12] This grotto is about thirty feet by forty feet and twelve to fifteen feet high. Today it contains a chapel and is located next to the Church of the Assumption. Twenty seven steps descend into its interior.
[13] We must learn to pray in amongst sleeping, lukewarm, and slothful Christians.
[14] So too must we pray when the Church, the body of Christ is attacked along with its members. Prayer is the weapon of choice.

The oppressive sins of the entire world now come in upon his soul like a great ocean of filth. Every sin has darkness and poison added to it by the evil spirits. Never before in the history of the world did the nearness of death bring such intense fear and anguish to any man as to this Blessed Man of Sorrows. Upon this most holy and purest of all beings came all the sins of the world in visions, from the fall of Adam and Eve to the last sin of the last person to ever live upon the earth.

There came to him all the back biting, selfishness, hateful and uncharitable thoughts actions and deeds. All the lying, deception, cheating, stealing, gossiping, false accusations and destructions of reputations. Every vile sin of envy and covetousness. The vile curses and oaths from foul mouths given over to hatred and all the sins perpetuated by hatred against the person. All the murder, abortions, euthanasia, unjust wars, oppression, persecution, kidnapping, slavery, usury and lack of forgiveness. All the blasphemies, sacrileges and schisms. All the impure filth of adultery, fornication, self abuse, same gender sex relations, bestiality plus all the impure desires, satisfactions and pleasures drawn from the sins of the flesh. He had to endure the rapists, molesters, sinful relationships and those who lure others into sinful relationships.

He saw the false teachers who destroy souls by leading them away from God. Every vile, abhorrent corruptive sin were heaped upon him as if they were all his own. [15]

Sin is the very object which weighs down his soul. This man of sorrows lying face down in the grotto has complete and perfect knowledge of all the hideous malice of sin and all the infinite displeasure, indignation and anger it awakens in his Heavenly Father. His perfectly pure nature is completely opposed to sin. Even the slightest of sins is completely abhorrent

---

[15] Picture yourself placed in a large vat, when suddenly every rotten vile element you can imagine is heaped upon you. Human and animal feces, urine, vomit, rotted flesh, maggots, skunk perfume, slime, corrosive chemicals, etc; heaped over your head and face until you could no longer stand above it as it was forced into your nose mouth and eyes until you were suffocating in it. Then you might begin to understand in a very imperfect way what was happening to Our Most Pure Lord as all sin was heaped upon him.

to his nature. He is overwhelmed with sadness and sorrow at the sight of all this filth and corruption. He is crushed to the ground by the intolerable sense of hatred his Eternal Father has for sin and for the sins of a sinful race to which he belongs and has chosen to represent.

The wrath of God is upon him; all the wrath that The Eternal Father has for sin is now directed upon the Son, the wrath that should be directed at us is now upon Our Redeemer because in his infinite love he takes it willingly upon himself. He, whom The Father has loved from all eternity; he whom has only known deep abiding love from The Father, a love beyond our ability to understand; he in whom The Father is well pleased is now the object of The Father's withering wrath for our sake. Neither human nor angelic minds are capable of understanding the anguish, pain and sorrow this causes Our Lord.

As The Son of God he is sinless. As The Messiah, The Christ, he is without sin. As the carpenter of Nazareth he is guilty of nothing. As the representative of the human race of which he is willingly a part, he has chosen to put on the sinful garment of his race in order to bring down upon himself the curse of this sinful race. For love of us he is become sin. He is to pay back the entire debt due from sinners. He knows only too well the amount of punishment these sins deserve. He is completely overwhelmed with sorrow. Willingly he takes all these sins unto himself as if he alone had committed them and offers himself to his Heavenly Father as just payment for the awful debt demanded by Divine Justice for satisfaction.

Satan himself now enters the grotto filled with diabolical joy at the sight of all the horrible sins of mankind and shows him even more vile visions of sinfulness. At the same time he shows Our Lord these sins he chides him; "Do you take even this sin upon yourself? Showing him ever more sinfulness he says; "Are you willing to bear its penalty?" Showing him a multitude of vile actions he sneers; "Are you prepared to satisfy for all of these?"[16]

---

[16] Quotes from the dolorous passion of Christ by Anne Catherine Emmerich.

23

Angels suddenly descended from Heaven to strengthen and invigorate him. As soon as the Angels departed Satan continued his onslaught.

He accused Our Lord of a great many crimes using events out of his life which he greatly distorted. He reproaches Our Lord with all the faults of his Disciples such as causing scandal by giving up ancient customs. He laid upon Our Lord the responsibility for the deaths of the holy innocents in Bethlehem after his birth. He blamed him for all the suffering his parents had to endure as a result of his coming into the world. He accused him of just letting John the Baptist die. He charged him with bringing disunity to families and protecting men of despicable character. He reminded him how he had caused injury to the people of gergesa by sending his demons into their swine herd which rushed down into the sea and drowned. He told him he had deserted his family and squandered their property.

On and on the accusations continued hoping to cause Our Lord to waver. Satan suggested to him every thought with which he would tempt an ordinary mortal at the hour of death that might have performed all his accusatory actions. It was still hidden from Satan that he was the Son of God. He tempted him only as the most just among men.

Our Lord was pleased to endure these temptations with which holy souls are assailed at the hour of their death concerning the merits of their good works. He permitted these temptations so that he might drink the chalice of suffering to the dregs.

Through all his temptations and sufferings Our Lord continued to pray and as time passes he becomes more terrified at the sight of the terrible endless crimes of mankind and their insufferable ingratitude toward God. His anguish is so great that he shudders and trembles and cries out; Father if is possible, remove this chalice from me. Father all things are possible to you, remove this chalice from me; nevertheless not my will but yours be done."

His love had insisted that he be left to all the weaknesses of his human nature. He was surrounded by frightful figures, sin, wickedness, vices and the ingratitude of mankind and all this was torturing and crushing him to the earth. He trembled and shuddered at the horror and terror of his approaching death. He fell from side to side, writhing like an injured worm because of his untold anguish. His entire body was bathed in a cold sweat.

In his prayer he had used the word chalice; "remove this chalice from me." Hebrews commonly used the word chalice to signify anything that required great labor or pain. To die for his friends and all those who would come to salvation was long desired by Our Lord but to die for the infidel, the reprobate, the ungrateful and contemptuous sinful souls who would not respond to his passion and death; those souls who would refuse to respond to his clemency and condemn themselves to eternal woe was what Our Lord called a chalice. This chalice was immensely bitter for Our Lord. He entered into an intense conflict between his Sacred Humanity and his Divinity. He was pleading that as his redemption would be super abundant for all, that no one, if possible should be lost. His Sacred Humanity, in its love for mankind, which were of his own nature, desired that all should gain eternal salvation by his passion and death.

St Michael the Archangel appeared to him in the name of the Eternal Father to tell him what in the depths of his soul he already knew; that it was not possible to save the unwilling. That even though the number who would willingly choose salvation was smaller than those who would not, the number was still great and that among them was his Most Holy Mother, the most worthy of all the redeemed. He also told him that the graces lost by the unwilling would be given more abundantly to those who would profit from his redemptive act through the fruits of his impassioned pleas for sinners.

If what he desired was not possible, in the end he would resign himself to it. He also had prayed that his blood should pass from him quickly so that there would be no delay in the salvation of mankind which he greatly desired but if this was not to be he would accept that also.

His sorrow was extremely bitter and he was terrified. The horrible visions never left him and he was overcome with sadness and anxiety. He rose to his feet but his legs were weak and his knees would barely keep him upright. He was pale and ashen and his features were noticeably altered. Shaking and trembling he began to climb out of the grotto. With a great degree of difficulty he came out into the open air, crossed the Bethany Road and stumbled over the earthen wall into the Garden of Olives. Staggering and wobbling he made his way up to the three Apostles. He was exhausted with fatigue, sorrow and anxiety. He had come to them seeking a little comfort from his friends for his overbearing sorrow. Also as a good shepherd he was concerned about them as he knew that they were also being tried by suffering and temptation.

He found them sleeping. He clasped his hands together in deep disappointment and sank to his knees beside them. In a shaking voice he said; "Simon, are you asleep?" The Apostles woke with a start and were horrified at the sight of him. They raised him to his feet and he lightly admonished them saying; "could you not watch one hour with me?" The Apostles didn't know what to say or think. They were astonished at what a pitiful trembling sight he had become. His voice had changed becoming almost inaudible. If he had not been surrounded by his well known halo of light they would not have recognized him.

John said; "Master what has happened to you? Shall I call the others? Our Lord answered; "If I were to live another thirty three years longer it would not be enough time to accomplish what must be fulfilled in me by this time tomorrow. Do not call the other eight. I did not bring them here because they could not bear to see me this way. If they did, they would give in to temptation, forget much of what they have seen in the past and lose faith in me. But you, who have seen The Son of Man transfigured, are also permitted to see him forsaken and suffering. Even so watch and pray that you will not fall into temptation, for the spirit is willing but the flesh is weak. My enemies and your enemies do not sleep as you do." [17]

Our Lord knew that Satan and his cohorts had also turned their attention to his Apostles as they were suspicious that they had received some great favor back at the cenacle. They intended

---

[17] Quote from the Dolorous Passion of Our Lord Jesus Christ by Anne Catherine Emmerich.

to learn what it was so they could counteract it. Our Lord seeing the cruel plans of the powers of darkness had hastened to his Apostles to rouse and encourage them to watch and pray in order that they might not be left unaware and unprovided for during these threatening temptations from their enemies. In his overwhelming sorrow he remained with his Apostles nearly fifteen minutes.

Then he turned back down the hill once again and started back to the grotto. The Apostles watch in stunned silence as he teetered and stumbled his way back to the grotto and went inside. They wept and embraced each other. "What can it be?" they said. "What is happening to him? He appears to be in a state of complete desolation." [18] They sat back down, covered their heads and prayed sorrowfully and anxiously.

The other eight Apostles who had stayed in the other section of the garden were at first unable to sleep. Our Blessed Savior's last words to them were so filled with suffering and sadness that they could not shake the feeling that something bad was about to happen. They searched all about Mount Olivet looking for a hiding place in case some danger should arise.

Once back into the grotto Our Lord fell face down upon the ground and prayed to his Heavenly Father. He rose up from his prayer as Angels came into him and in a series of terrible visions showed him in exact detail all the horrible sufferings he would have to endure to atone for sin. They showed him the beauty of mankind before the fall and how sin had altered and destroyed that beauty. They showed him how all sin had originated in the sin of Adam. Then they showed him the extraordinary sufferings he would have to endure for the sins of lust alone. He reacted with extreme horror and was so overwhelmed by the terrible satisfaction that would be required to atone for the vile sins of adultery, fornication, same gender sex, bestiality, self abuse and lustful and sexual fantasies of every kind. The abuse of marriage, which he had elevated to a sacrament, through divorce, remarriage and the mockery of

---

[18] Quote from the Dolorous Passion of Our Lord Jesus Christ by Anne Catherine Emmerich.

marriage by cohabitation and willfully preventing the birth of children by artificial and unnatural means. What an extremely high degree of suffering of body and soul would be needed for the atonement of these horrid sins which mankind so freely and callously enter into in complete opposition to the Divine Decree against them. Sins for which he knows that more souls earn for themselves eternal punishment in hell than for any other sin. The Angels showed him all these things under different forms. All this horrible debt had to be paid by that Sacred Humanity which alone was guilty of no sin.

No tongue has ever uttered the words; no words have ever come into existence which could even begin to describe the horror and anguish which crushed Our Lord's most pure, innocent and holy soul at the sight of the terrible payback that was due to satisfy for the sins of impurity and lust. Those sins in which mankind takes so much false and phony momentary pleasure with no thought to their own state of grace, to his commandants and their own ruin for all eternity. His agony was so great that a bloody sweat came forth from every pore in his body and soaked his garments. The Angels withdrew from him.

Next, he was beaten down by the prospect of the ingratitude of mankind to his passion and death. He contemplated the future sufferings of his Mystical Body, The Church which would be brought about by the coming persecutions of his Apostles, Disciples and friends. He also foresaw the horrific errors, schisms and heresies that would be brought about by the children of The Church due to pride and disobedience. He contemplated the evil, corruption and lack of sincerity that would plague those who would call themselves Christians down through the ages. He beheld with great sadness the lies and deceptions of false teachers; the sacrilege's of wicked Priests and religious and the fatal consequences of all these sins.

He saw the abominations and desolations in the sanctuaries of his Church by the same ungrateful mankind he was about to redeem with unspeakable suffering. He contemplated every kind of fanaticism, obstinacy and evil perpetuated by the minds of mankind in the form of apostates, heresiarchs and pretended reformers who would deceive the faithful by the phony appearance of sanctity. He saw them competing with each other, tearing at the very fabric of his Church by insults, ill treatment and outright denial. Many had turned away from him shaking their heads at him and his teachings. Many in the future would do the same and he foresaw it all. Avoiding his compassionate embrace they would ignore all that he was suffering for them and plunge head long with great haste into the eternal abyss.

He foresaw that many of those who would not deny him would merely look on with disgust and with indifference as his Church was torn and assailed. He contemplated his true Church deserted by much of mankind through cowardice and lack of faith allowing themselves to be separated from the true vine by false doctrines and by teachers ignoring his true Church. He saw them building their own churches, not his, on the sands of false doctrine which they constantly changed. These churches had neither altar nor sacrifice as he had commanded. In their incessant error they constantly attacked the true Church. Darkness dwelt in these churches as they only barely retained some spiritual life by retaining some of the doctrines of his true Church which greatly diminished their access to grace. They obstinately refused to enter into the truth because they feared the sacrifices which truth demands. In their blindness these churches abandoned his greatest gift, the gift of himself in the Eucharist. They walked away from his greatest grace and the great sacrifice he was making on their behalf. He beheld all the ingratitude and corruption of all Christians of all ages until the end of the world.

During all the time he was being shown the ingratitude of mankind Satan incessantly chided him saying; "can you resolve to suffer for these ungrateful reprobates? Can you suffer for these? Can you take upon yourself even these sins?" [19] His soul was heavily weighed down and crushed. His Sacred Humanity was despoiled by unspeakable anguish. He writhed from side to side and clasped his hands together as he sank to the ground beneath the weight of his horrible suffering.

---

[19] Quote from the Dolorous Passion of Jesus Christ by Anne Catherine Emmerich.

He entered into a violent struggle with his human will and its aversion to suffer for such an ungrateful race. This struggle was so intense and traumatic that from every pore in his body there came forth large drops of blood which formed into clots and trickled onto the ground. [20] His anguish was so great that he raised his voice and emitted several cries and groans of pain. His cries were so loud that he awoke the Apostles in the Garden of Olives. Peter leaped up and ran to the grotto. Pushing the vegetation aside he looked in and said; "Master, what has befallen you?" [21] At the pitiful sight of his Lord drenched in blood, Peter drew back and paused for a moment, rendered motionless by terror. Our lord did not answer him or even give any indication that he had seen him. Peter ran back to James and John and told them what he had witnessed. Once again they sat on the ground, covered their heads and tried to pray.

The horrible visions of future ingratitude became more vivid and ever worse. Our Lord cried out several times;"Oh my Father can I possibly suffer for such an ungrateful race? Oh my Father, if this chalice cannot pass from me unless I drink it, thy will be done". During all these visions Satan continued to hold a noticeable place in all types of hideous forms.

Satan disappeared and many of his demons took his place. Our Lord saw them tear to pieces and drag away many of

---

[20] St Luke, writing in the Greek text uses the word; "thromboi" which translates into clot. These clots have always presented translators with problems as they contend, and correctly so, that clots cannot come out of the body. So some have changed or omitted the word clot because they do not understand the normal process. The medical term for blood sweating is haematidrosis. In times of great trauma the tiny blood vessels beneath the skin called capillaries swell causing them to burst when they come into contact with the millions of sweat glands which exist all over the body. The blood mingles with the sweat and comes out the pores. Once outside the body the blood coagulates and becomes clots which fall to the ground during a profuse sweat. Such a hemorrhage would not only reduce the body's resistance but would cause the entire surface of the skin to become tender and painful to the touch, let alone to blows. Pierre Barbet, M.D. Forensic Pathologist, in his book; "A doctor at Calvary".
[21] Quote from the Dolorous Passion of Our Lord Jesus Christ by Anne Catherine Emmerich.

those for whom he was about to enter upon the painful way of the cross. None of these frightful figures resembled any known creature but were demonical to the fullest extent. They were symbols of abomination, discord, sin and contradiction.

Satan soon returned in the form of a large reptile with a crown on his head and seemed to be possessed of a great deal of strength. He brought with him countless legions of the enemies of Our Lord from every age and nation armed with all kinds of destructive weapons. Sometimes they tore each other to pieces then renewed their attacks on Our Lord with double the rage. They directed at him the most fearful outrages while cursing at him and striking and tearing at him with their weapons, swords and spears. The rage of each and every sinner was directed at Our Lord and he was deeply wounded just as if every blow had been real. Satan, being in the middle of the onslaught beat the ground with his tail tearing to pieces and devouring all those he knocked down and took away from Our Lord.

All these sinners who had been presented before Our Lord and who were afflicting him with such great sorrows, were all those who down through the ages would outrage him in his Blessed Sacrament; his precious body, blood, soul and divinity; the most precious gift of himself in which he would remain present among mankind until the consummation of the world, solely out of his deep burning love for us.

They were outraging him through neglect, irreverence, omission of honor due to him, open contempt, abuse and outright sacrilege. Through worship of earthly idols and luxuries by those who loved the world to the exclusion of their God. Through outrageous and irreverent service at his altar by not properly honoring him during sacred ceremonies. By sacrilegious Priests, many of whom firmly believe themselves to be full of faith and piety but were outrageous to Our Lord in the Blessed Sacrament.

By the blind, paralyzed, deaf and dumb people who would refuse to acknowledge his presence on the altar, refusing to receive him, refusing to defend his real presence in the sacred species and thereby refusing to move along the road to eternal salvation.

Many who believed and taught the doctrine of the real presence did not really take it to heart themselves and neglected the throne, the palace and the seat of the Living God by demeaning the importance of the Church, the altar, the tabernacle, the chalice, the monstrance and all items used in worship or to adorn his house.

He saw churches fall into dishonor and disuse. The worship of God was, if not inwardly profaned, outwardly dishonored. He saw his churches empty, dirty and adorned with worldly, tasteless and unsuitable ornaments which replaced magnificent adornments of a more pious age. He saw the adorable sacrament profaned, churches deserted, Priests despised even by many of the faithful who approached the altar to receive him with the tabernacle of their heart unprepared to welcome him; filled instead with filth and corruption.

He foresaw that the private lodgings of many would be far better than the lodgings provided for him and in many cases his throne, the tabernacle which was shunted to an out of the way place where it was afforded little reverence.

He saw the rise of indifference, sloth, egotism and preoccupation with vain earthly concerns to the outright neglect of all things spiritual. He was deeply grieved at the lack of hospitality shown by mankind to whom he was to give himself as food; food for the soul; living bread come down from Heaven; food that satisfies unto all eternity.

He foresaw wicked soldiers profaning sacred vessels and even saw his holy and Blessed Sacrament used in satanic worship. He saw theologians drawn to heresy by their sins, attacking him in the Eucharist and leading souls astray. He saw large chunks of his mystical body the Church, torn away in rejection of the Eucharist, just as other Disciples had walked away from him when he first announced that he would give his body and blood as real food for all mankind. His unifying body, blood, soul and divinity in the Eucharist which should have made all of mankind as one had become the vehicle of separation because of lack of faith and false teaching.

He witnessed entire nations flee him depriving themselves of that sanctifying vessel of grace left to the Church.

Having separated themselves from his life giving Church they fell into errors of infidelity, superstition and heresy and became prey to the false defiling philosophies of the world. Urged on by Satan who was in the midst of them, they banded together in large bodies to assail and denounce the true Church, his very own mystical body.

The blood was flowing in large droplets down the sides of his sacred face and his beard and hair were completely matted. He staggered out of the grotto and made his way to the Garden of Olives. As he approached the Apostles he was trembling badly and his moans and groans were so loud that he awoke them as he came near, for they had again fallen asleep. He was so altered in appearance that they did not immediately recognize him. They rose up and supported him as he was so feeble and weakened that they though he would fall.

With deep sorrow he told them that he would be put to death on the next day. That he would be seized within one hour's time, be led before tribunals, mistreated, outraged, scourged and put to a most cruel death. He asked them to console his Mother and Mary Magdalene. [22] The Apostles said nothing as they did not know what to say to him at this time. They though his mind had been affected.

When he desired to return to the grotto he no longer had the strength to walk on his own. James and John had to help him return to the grotto. As soon as Our Lord went in they returned to the Garden of Olives.

The other eight Apostles ended their search for a hiding place and returned to the area of the arbor. In their anxiety they began to discuss among themselves what they should do once Our Lord had been put to death. They had given up everything to follow him and now they were counted among the poor and

---

[22] Our Lord was touched by Magdalene's anguish. He knew that her love for him was greater than anyone else other than his Most Holy Mother. He also knew that she would have to suffer a great deal for his sake and that she would not sin against him anymore. She had been forgiven much and she loved much.

despised of the world. After discussing this for some time, they fell asleep.

Many of the Disciples who had also been in the cenacle that night had at first wandered off in different directions to attend to personal business but having heard about the dreadful prophecies of Our Lord they left Jerusalem and went to the town of Bethpage on the northern slope of Mount Olivet.

Once back in the grotto the repugnance of Our Lord's humanity to suffer returned. He at once abandoned himself to the will of his Heavenly Father. The earth opened before him and he saw the abode of the just who had already died and were awaiting his arrival in the lower world. Adam and Eve, his mother's parents, his foster father Joseph, John the Baptist, the patriarchs and prophets and all the just who had died and had not merited damnation. His death would open Heaven to all these captives. When he looked upon these saints in waiting it gave courage and strength to his adoring heart.

Angels came to him once again and showed to him the future saints of the Church, who themselves joining their efforts to his passion were to be united through him to his Heavenly Father. He beheld a beautiful vision of salvation and sanctity bursting forth in ceaseless streams from the fountain of redemption unleashed by his passion and death. There appeared before him the entire army of the blessed, the Apostles, the Disciples, Virgins, Holy women, martyrs, confessors, hermits, Popes, Bishops, Priests, Religious and the countless number of the faithful who would obtain salvation from that glorious redemptive fountain. All wore crowns which differed in form, order, color and perfection according to the sufferings, labors and victories which had won them eternal life. The whole of their lives, actions, merits and powers plus the glory of their triumph came entirely from their union with him through his passion and death.

The past army and the future army of the saints joined together to give a large degree of comfort to the soul of the Redeemer. Oh, how he loved these creatures. He so loved his brethren that he would have gladly given himself up to the same passion and death to accomplish the redemption of one single solitary soul.

The comforting visions now left him. One more time the Angels showed him every part of the passion he was about to endure in minute detail. He also saw and felt the suffering endured by his Most Holy Mother whose interior union with his sufferings was so complete that she fainted into the arms of her companions. The visions ended and the Angels left him. He fell on his face like someone about to die. The grotto was now completely dark and he was alone.

After a while he rose up and St Michael the Archangel appeared before him dressed in long flowing robes similar to a Priest. He placed a morsel of food in Our Lord's mouth and gave him a chalice to drink. Then he disappeared. [23]

Our Lord remained in the grotto for a little while longer absorbed in calm meditation giving thanks to his Eternal Father. He was still in deep affliction of spirit. By deliberate and eternal forethought he had chosen to sacrifice himself for us. He has resolved to deliver himself up to sorrow, anguish and death because he places a higher value on the treasure he wishes to redeem then on the price he intends to pay. [24]

The visit by St Michael has strengthened him to such a degree that he is able to leave the grotto without staggering. He wiped his face and straightened his hair as best he could even though his hair was still matted with blood. He went to his three Apostles and once again found them sleeping. He said to them: "Are you still sleeping and taking your rest? Now is not the time for sleep. Arise and pray. Behold the hour is at hand and the Son of Man will be betrayed into the hands of sinners. Arise, let us go. Behold he is at hand that will betray me. It was better for him if that man had not been born."

---

[23] This action of St Michael did not diminish his sorrow but increased it. He was strengthened so that he might be able to suffer even more for the love of mankind and the glory of his Eternal Father. All the sufferings of the entire passion were present to him in the garden.

[24] He knew that he would not be able to suffer these pains any more after his death, so he drank the chalice of suffering in advance, in this garden, which he now made holy by blessing it with his precious blood.

The three Apostles arose and looked anxiously around. Our Lord pointed out to them the band of armed men in the valley across the brook Kidron coming toward the Garden of Gethsemane with light torches. He spoke calmly and once again asked them to console his Mother. Then Our Lord said; "Let us go to meet them. I will deliver myself up without resistance into the hands of my enemies". [25]

They left the Garden of Olives and went out to the Gethsemane road and positioned themselves in front of the arbor which was on the road between the Garden of Olives and the cultivated garden in which he had left the other eight Apostles.

Throughout the passion of Our Lord in the garden and the grotto, his Most Holy Mother remained in the Cenacle with the holy women who always accompanied her. Through Divine permission she saw clearly in visions all that took place during Our Lord's agony. As co-redemptrix, her actions during the agony completely mirrored those of her Divine Son. When Our Lord separated himself from the eight and took Peter, James and John with him, she separated herself from the main body of women and took Magdalene, Mary Cleophus and Mary the mother of Mark with her. She cautioned the main body of women to watch and pray that they may not fall victim to temptation. Of the three Mary's she took with her into another part of the Cenacle, she treated Magdalene as head of the rest the same as Our Lord treated Peter.

The Blessed Virgin begged the Eternal Father to suspend all human relief and comfort in not only the human portion of her being but also in the soul so that she could suffer to the highest degree in union with her Divine Son. She wished to feel in her own immaculate body all the torments that he would feel. The Holy Trinity granted this petition and decreed that the Immaculate Virgin would suffer all the torments that her Son would suffer in exact proportion. In her most burning love it would have been more terrible for her to behold the suffering of her Divine Son without being allowed to share in his agony.

---

[25] Quote from the Dolorous Passion of Our Lord Jesus Christ by Anne Catherine Emmerich.

The Queen of love instructed the three Mary's to assist her during her affliction and because of this they were given greater understanding and grace that the other women.

When Our Lord was confessing to his three Apostle that; "his soul was sorrowful unto death", she confessed to the three Mary's; "My soul is sorrowful because my beloved Son is about to suffer and die of his torments. Pray that you may not be overcome by temptation".

She then went away from the three into a garden connected to the house and followed along with Our Lord in all his supplications, praying in as much as it was possible for her and enduring the same agonies as he was enduring in the grotto.

Each time her Son returned to his Apostles, she returned to the three women to encourage them because she knew of the wrath of the demon against them.

During the agony she wept bitterly over the loss of all reprobates as she was given enlightenment concerning the mysteries of predestination and the unrepentant sinner.

During the intervals when St Michael appeared to Our Lord, St Gabriel the Archangel appeared to her with the same messages. Our Holy Lady also endured bloody sweats at the same intervals of that of her Divine Son. She fell prostrate with grief as she beheld the depths of the agonies of Our Lord.

At length she sent Angelic messengers to the garden to inquire concerning her Divine Son but because of her deep anxieties she did not await their return. Along with the three Mary's she went toward Gethsemane as far as the Kidron Valley. She again beheld Our Lord, in a vision, enduring a bloody sweat and sent Angels of her guard to wipe his tormented face. Out of love for his holy Mother, Our Lord allowed the Angels to fulfill her wish and clean his face.

Some of the wandering Disciples saw Our Lady and the three Mary's in the valley and seeing that the soldiers were approaching hurriedly took them back to the Cenacle.

Chapter II
The Arrest

Judas was sick of the apostolic life. He was fed up with moving about constantly and being harassed by the authorities. He had been under the impression that Our Lord would set up an earthly kingdom in which he would command a position of authority and wealth. He came to the decision that what he had dreamed and hoped for was probably not going to happen and he began to think of ways to obtain wealth on his own. His greed had been on the increase for quite awhile and he had been stealing from the apostolic purse which was in his charge.

Judging from what he saw taking place around him, he came to the opinion that Our Lord was headed for trouble and decided that he had better make friends with those in authority before the situation got out of hand. Our Lord had not become King as he had hoped but the High Priest already had plenty of dignity and power and so did those who were in his service. This impressed the wicked heart of Judas and he managed to get himself connected with some of the High Priest's staff members. Eventually he was introduced to Annas, the former High Priest and then to Joseph Ciaphas the reigning High Priest.

Even though Judas had gone to great lengths to make himself known to those in power and seek their friendship, they did not treat him well and could not bring themselves to trust him completely.

The ruling class was of the opinion that now was not a good time to move against Our Lord due to the closeness of the festival of Passover. There would be pilgrims in Jerusalem from all over the world and an arrest at this time would draw too much attention. They preferred to wait until the feast was over.

Satan, being a part of these deliberations with his temptations and suggestions to these wicked plotters could not make up his own mind. He wanted Our Lord killed, that was definite. Even if this holy Rabbi was just a good man, he was converting too many souls and he thoroughly despised him. On the other hand he had a bad feeling about seeking the death of this man who would not hide himself or flee from his enemies. He needed to know who he really was. He finally decided to play both sides in that he would tempt Our Lord's enemies to deep hatred and fury against him while suggesting at the same time to others that Judas was not to be trusted and that all should be delayed until after the festival.

Judas was fully aware by now that he had not succeeded in winning their trust as the speech and actions of the authorities gave away their true feelings. To gain their trust he offered to give back his thirty pieces of silver to the Temple treasury to convince them that his intentions were above reproach. They refused his offer telling him that the price of blood could not be deposited into the Temple treasury by law. Seeing how much they hated him made Judas flush with anger. This is not what he had hoped for; he was not making friends in high places as he had desired but he had gone this far with them in their evil planning and he was now in their control.

He assured the plotters that Our Lord was alone with the eleven Apostles and that all of them were downcast and troubled. He told them that the eleven were timid men and would not defend their Master. He strongly urged them that now was the time to affect the arrest as he had no intention of returning to his service and could be of no use to them in the future.

They observed Judas closely and thought about his suggestions. Then they insisted that he show them precisely what needed to be done to capture him this very night. He advised them to take great precautions to make sure that Our Lord would not be able to escape by use of some magic or miracle as he had done in the past.

Finally listening to the arguments of Judas, they began to plot the best way to carry out their evil designs to secure his arrest as soon as possible. They had at their disposal a large number of soldiers who were Temple guards and directly under the command of the High Priest. They consisted of many Jews but were mostly pagan mercenaries who were employed to keep order in the vast Temple area and anywhere else the High Priest required their services. They wore uniforms similar to but not quite the same as those of the Roman soldiers. They decided that three hundred soldiers would line the streets from the compound of the High Priest's on Mount Zion to the eastern gate at Ophel which leads into the Kidron Valley. In this way they hoped to keep under control any persons which might be friendly to Our Lord once they had him in custody. They would also remain on alert, to go to the aid of the arresting band if needed.

The arresting band would consist of twenty more soldiers armed with spears, swords, clubs and staves carrying torches and lanterns to illume the night. They would be accompanied by four military bailiffs [26] and six agents of the High Priest who had former dealings with Judas. They consisted of four Pharisees, one Herodian and one Sadducee. All six of these agents despised Our Lord and had longed for his arrest for quite some time. They were to supervise the apprehension.

Judas warned them that every precaution must be taken to prevent his escape through the use of miraculous powers so the bailiffs checked and rechecked all their chains, cords and leather belts to be sure they left nothing behind that would be needed to securely bind him.

Before setting out to the garden of Gethsemane they insisted that Judas return to the Cenacle to check and be certain that Our Lord had not returned there. Three Pharisees went with him and not finding Our Lord there decided that he must be on Mount Olivet as Judas had stated. Returning to the compound of the High Priests they made final preparations for the arrest.

As soon as they assured themselves that all was in order to properly secure his apprehension, the arresting band set out with all their equipment in the direction of Mount Olivet. The three hundred soldiers followed close behind, taking up their positions on each side of the street as they went.

Observing all these proceedings from her place in the Cenacle the Holy Mother of God could foresee the lack of reverence and multiple insults that were about to be heaped upon

---

[26] The bailiffs were servants of the High Priest who were most assuredly part of the Temple Guard which dealt mainly with matter of the ruling council or Sanhedrin.

her Divine Son by this band of soldiers now leaving the city to affect his arrest. She at once asked the Holy Angels of her guard and the women who accompanied her to give praise and adoration to their Divine Lord to offset the abominations he was about to endure at the hands of wicked men.

Our Lord and his three Apostles stood in the moonlight beneath the arbor in the Gethsemane road facing the city. Our Lord pointed out to them the movement of the arresting band as they crossed over the Kidron and headed in their direction. Peter expressed his desire to fight arguing that the other eight were close at hand and that they could all mount an attack. Our Lord would not allow it.

The other eight Apostles were awakened by the noise of the approaching soldiers and joined Our Lord at the Arbor. Our Lord once again gave instructions to his Apostles and warned them again of all that was about to take place.

Then with deep love and piety he prayed interiorly; "Oh sufferings, longingly desired from my inmost soul; pains, wounds, affronts, labors, afflictions and humiliating death, come, come, come quickly. For the fire of love which burns for the salvation of men is anxious to see you meet the innocent one of all creatures. Well do I know your value! I have sought, desired and solicited you and I meet you joyously of my own free will. I have purchased you by my anxiety in searching for you and I esteem you for your merits. I desire to remedy and enhance your value and raise you to the highest dignity. Let death come, in order that by my accepting it I may triumph over it and gain life for those who have been punished by death for their sins. I give permission for my friends to forsake me; for I alone desire and am able to enter into this battle and gain for them triumph and victory." [27]

The soldiers acted somewhat friendly to Judas until they reached the intersection of the Bethany Road and the Gethsemane Road at the base of Mount Olivet. Then an argument arose between them as Judas wanted to go on ahead alone to give the impression that he was not part of the arresting

---

[27] Quote from the city of God by Mary of Agreda.

41

band but just happened to be arriving on the Mount at the same time by sheer coincidence. The soldiers were not about to let him out of their sight as they did not trust him and started to act hostile toward him, refusing to allow him to advance. They had no intention of letting Judas go until they had their prisoner secured.

While they were still arguing, Our Lord in union with all his Apostles approached them [28] and while they were still arguing said to them in a clear firm voice; "whom do you seek?" One of the agents answered; "Jesus of Nazareth." Manifesting his Divinity and speaking with Divine authority Our Lord replied; "I am He!" When they had heard these words, the twenty soldiers, the horses and dogs they had brought with them became powerless and fell backward to the ground. They lay motionless as if they were dead. Judas, the four bailiffs and the six agents did not fall as they were already in the power of Satan. However, Satan and his cohorts, being present were also thrown down and held motionless, suffering great confusion.

Our Blessed Mother, witnessing all this from her place in the Cenacle sang a canticle in the company of her Angels, praising the infinite power of her Divine Son and the glorious dignity of his sacred humanity.

While the soldiers, animals and demons lay immobile, Our Lord said to Judas; "Friend, why have you come?" He sent grace into the heart of Judas so that he could understand clearly the evil of his treason while at the same time showing him the punishment he would have to endure if he did not sincerely repent of his present course and accept the forgiveness offered by his clemency. Judas mumbled something about some unattended business which had brought him to the garden. Our Lord told him that it would be better for him if he had never been born.

---

[28] By advancing in one body to confront his enemies, Our Lord and his Apostles formed the first Mystical Union and in so doing, Our Lord showed his Apostles how they were to approach the enemies of the Church. If they wished to defeat the demons and evil enemies they must do it in perfect union.

The soldiers were beginning to regain their strength and were slowly getting to their feet. [29] They timidly began to approach but made no attempt to affect an arrest. They were waiting for Judas to give them the prearranged sign so they would have positive identification of the man they had orders to apprehend.

The Apostles gathered around Judas and began to vent their anger at him for his treachery. Judas made an attempt to calm them down by trying to lie his way out of this predicament but the truth became apparent when the soldiers offered to come to his defense. The Apostles continued to verbally assault Judas expressing their anger at his shameful and unspeakable act of treason toward their Master.

Again Our Lord asked them; "whom do you seek?" They replied once more; "Jesus of Nazareth." Again Our Lord said; "I have told you that I am he! If therefore, you seek me, let these men go their way. The soldiers withdrew back a few steps and fell once again to the ground this time writhing and convulsing involuntarily.

The Holy Mother was witness to both falls of the soldiers and again sang songs of praise to the infinite power of her Divine Son and of the virtues of his humanity in union with the Angels of her guard. She praised him with great fervor because he was about to deliver himself up to rescue all humanity from the bonds of Satan. She then prayed to her Divine Son to let all those who were lying helpless to regain their senses and be allowed to get to their feet. She was asking out of her most generous love and compassion even for those who were about to arrest and persecute him. She was also fulfilling to the highest degree his command to love and do good to your enemies. She was also aware of the prophecies of Holy Scripture which must be satisfied to redeem this fallen race.

With deep sadness in his heart Our Lord looked upon these men who were contemplating their foul deeds and so steeped in their immense hatred. Eternal damnation expressed itself in all their actions and behaviors. By this miracle and

---

[29] Not so for the animals and demons.

display of Divine power he wished to show his great love for his friends and to his enemies he was giving a last chance at conversion.

He now prayed to his Eternal Father saying: "My Father and Eternal God, into my hands you have placed all things and consigned to me the redemption required by your justice. I wish to satisfy it and give myself over to death with all my heart in order to merit for my brethren participation in your treasure and eternal happiness held out to them." [30]

Our Lord had made the rising of all who had been thrown down solely dependant on the intercession of his Blessed Mother. Answering the prayer of his Mother, he now allows all of them to get up, saying to them; "arise." Animals, demons and soldiers are now allowed to become mobile again.

Satan, being allowed to rise immediately held a conference with his cohorts saying; "this cannot possibly be the work of a mere human but one who is both God and man. If he is, he will redeem man and satisfy God's justice. Our influence will be diminished and our plans defeated. We are making a mistake in wanting him killed. We must test his endurance. This is what we must do. Excite his enemies to cruel treatment and torture. Suggest to their minds the vilest of torments so as to try his patience severely while we study the results." [31]

Satan was still unsure of who he was dealing with. At times he thought him to be God but could not accept the fact that God could allow himself to be so humiliated without using miracles to prevent it.

Upon rising the soldiers were timid and still terrified. They told Judas to immediately give them the signal they had agreed on before leaving the city. Judas stepped forward and kissed Our Lord saying; "Hail Master." Our Lord had to bend down to received his blistering kiss as he was taller than Judas. Those foul treacherous lips were allowed to touch the face upon which Angels long to look. Those same lips the body, blood, soul and Divinity of Our Lord had passed through such a short time

---

[30] Quote from the City of God by Mary of Agreda.
[31] Quote from the City of God by Mary of Agreda.

before when Judas had received the Blessed Eucharist along with the other Apostles.

The Blessed Virgin in viewing this outrage prayed ardently to her Son and Lord to grant new graces to Judas to save his soul from damnation if he would choose to do so. In answer to her prayer he granted to Judas powerful graces at the very moment the kiss touched his face. If Judas would have responded to this grace obtained for him by the Mother of Mercy which was dispensed immediately by her Divine Son he would have obtained pardon for his sin. He did not and lost salvation.

Our Lord replied to Judas saying; "Judas, do you betray the Son of Man with a kiss?" Having received the sign, the soldiers immediately surrounded Our Lord but did not touch him. Judas attempted to flee but the Apostles would not allow it. A soldier named Malchus advanced toward the Savior and the Apostles cried out; "shall we strike with the sword?" Peter drew his sword and launched a mighty blow at the head of Malchus but it glanced off his helmet, caught his right ear and severed it from his head.

Our Lord said to Peter; "Put your sword back into its scabbard for all who take to the sword will perish with the sword." Do you not think that I could ask my Father and he would give me at once more than twelve legions of Angels? How then will the scriptures be fulfilled?" He went up to Malchus, touched his ear and prayed. Malchus was healed at once.

Those who were standing close by were unmoved by the miracle. They insulted Our Lord and said; "he uses witchcraft; this is a thing of the devil. He made the ear appeared to be cut off and now he used the same power to make it appear healed. [32]

Our Lord spoke to the arresting band once more in a firm clear voice: "You have come out as it were to a robber with swords and clubs to apprehend me. I sat with you daily teaching in the Temple and you did not lay hands on me; but this is your

---

[32] They were accusing him of inducing hallucinations. Quote from the Dolorous Passion of Our Lord Jesus Christ by Anne Catherine Emmerich.

hour and the power of darkness." [33] By saying these words Our Lord has now given permission to the band of thugs to take him prisoner, mistreat him and put him to death. He will offer no resistance from this point on.

His Holy Mother not only witnessed his capture as clearly as if she had been present but by means of supernatural visions was able to penetrate deeply into Our Lord's words and actions. She confided to her companions that her Divine Son had now given permission to his enemies to arrest and mistreat him and that they were now going to set about using this permission in a most cruel manner. [34]

The four bailiffs stepped forward and took hold of Our Lord. Using new cords, they roughly yanked his arms behind him and securely tied his left hand to his right elbow and his right hand to his left elbow causing much pain to his arms and shoulders. They clasped a leather belt around his waist and a leather collar around his neck. Leather straps were attached to the neck collar, crossed over his chest and attached to the leather belt. Then a chain was attached to the front of the belt, passed down through his groin area, pulled tightly up his back and wrapped around his neck, then down his front to the belt and fastened. This caused the head to be bent forward at all times with the chain rubbing constantly in the groin area making it very difficult to walk.

Still fearing that he might escape their clutches as he had done in the past, they bound him with a second heavy chain in such a manner that it encircled his waist, then his neck, leaving

---

[33] Our Lord is making one last effort to deter his enemies away from their wickedness by pointing out to them how unworthy their actions are in treating him as the worst of criminals. He reminds them that he spoke openly, showing himself to be a great benefactor to the people, not a danger. He reminds them that they could not take him captive no matter how many swords and clubs they have if he didn't allow it but this hour belongs to them along with the powers of darkness.

[34] It is noted that some readers may have a hard time coming to grips with the fact that the Blessed Virgin witnessed much of the passion in visions. God can do anything that man can do and more. We can witness events that take place in other parts of the world by way of tele "visions". If man can, God can!

the two ends of the chain dangling behind his back which were then attached to two large padlocked rings which were placed around his already tied hands to act as handcuffs. Then they tied another cord around his arms and fastened them to the waist belt behind him. Still not content they wound a heavy rope around his neck, crossed it over his chest, knotting it to the leather straps and waist belt, leaving two long ends in front to pull him with. Then they tied a second heavy rope to his shackled arms, secured it to the back of the waist belt leaving two long ends to his rear in order to pull on him from behind. It was in this manner that Our Lord allowed himself to be taken prisoner for the love of men.

When the bailiffs seized Our Lord and bound him so tightly, the Holy Mother felt all the pains caused by the ropes and chains in her own body as if she were being tied up and mistreated as well. She also felt the effects of all the blows and infirmities heaped upon her Divine Son by his malefactors. [35]

During the time of binding, Satan and his cohorts tempted and urged the bailiffs to ill treat Our Lord beyond all bounds of human decency. They were not only willing dupes of Satan but also the six Agents with whom they hoped to gain favor for they were fully aware that the agents hated and despised their captive. They gave rise to every kind of outrage against Our Lord using curses, vile language and blasphemies while striking him and treating him cruelly within the boundaries allowed by the Eternal Father.

Taking advantage of the arresting bands preoccupation in securing Our Lord, the Apostles ran away unnoticed. It was the intention of Our Lord not to allow them to be taken at this time as it was his hour, not theirs. The time for them to suffer would eventually come. When Our Lord had told the arresting band to let them go, he was not making a plea but issuing a Divine command.

Satan and his demons were hard at work trying to upset the Apostles with many suggestions while playing on their fears

---

[35] This effect in the body of Our Holy Mother will continue throughout the passion.

and confusion. [36] He wanted to see them all captured and killed so that the doctrines Our Lord preached would be stamped out completely. Understanding that this was not going to take place at this time, caused him to incite the Apostles to run away. He did not want them around to witness the extraordinary patience and virtue exhibited by Our Lord as he suffered. He did not want this to confirm and fortify their faith as it would make them better able to resist the temptations he planned to inflict on them. He reasoned that if he could weaken their resolve now, he would be in a better position to tempt them to fall away entirely, as Judas had, by way of the persecutions he had in store for them. When he determined that they were given over to fear, confusion and sorrow he assaulted them furiously with doubts about Our Lord and urged them to run.

Although the Apostles gave in to the temptation of Satan to run they resisted the temptation to lose faith in Our Lord. They scattered in different directions as they were afraid they could not hide as easily if they all remained together. Peter and John stayed together and remained at a distance from the garden to see what would happen to their Master.

As soon as Our Lord was tightly secured a runner was sent to the High Priest who immediately set into motion their wicked designs in receiving him. Guards were stationed at the entrances of all buildings and all rooms to be used were fully lighted. Messengers were dispatched to different parts of Jerusalem to alert all members of the assembly.[37] They needed to be present to take part in the trial. Many of them were already present as they had been waiting at the home of the High Priest since the deal had been made with Judas and the arresting band had departed for Mount Olivet to see whether or not the arresting band would be successful this time.

Due to the Passover festival there were many Elders, Pharisees, Sadducees and Herodians in Jerusalem from all over Israel. Many had waited a very long time to see the day when

---

[36] Our Lord had warned them many times to watch and pray because of these very temptations.
[37] Know as the Sanhedrin.

Our Lord would be arrested. The High Priest was now sending messengers especially to those members who were hostile enemies of Our Lord advising them to bring all evidence which they had against him to present to the tribunal. Many of these haughty leaders of the people from all parts of the country had been publicly admonished by Our Lord and had been dying for a chance to avenge themselves.

Messengers were sent out to the inns where these leaders were staying and to all the homes of the local dignitaries to assure their appearance at this hastily arranged trial. They sent for the Temple merchants who had been assaulted and driven out by him. They called for the doctors of the law who had been publicly humiliated by him, some who had held grudges from as far back as when Our Lord had corrected them in the Temple precincts when he was only twelve years old. They rounded up unconverted sinners whom he had refused to cure and some whose ailments had returned when they fell back into a life of sin. Worldly and sinful men whom he had rejected as Disciples and anyone that would like to see an end to his ministry were also summoned.

The arresting band was finally satisfied with his bonds, so they lit fresh torches and proceeded to get underway to return to the city. Ten soldiers led the procession while the four bailiffs manned the ropes. The six agents stayed close to him so they could torment and demean him. The other ten soldiers brought up the rear of the column.

They came out of the garden shouting, laughing and congratulating each other on the capture of this elusive man who had always avoided their clutches in the past. They blasphemed, cursed and reviled him with every step. The two bailiffs in the front cruelly pulled him forward while the two in the rear pulled back on him to retard his steps. At times they made him run forward causing him to fall and at other times they jerked him backward violently. They also pulled him from side to side making it difficult for him to keep his balance.

On several occasions he was thrown to the ground with great force. With his hands tightly secured behind him he was unable to break his falls and his face became severely bruised

49

and riddled with cuts. When he fell, they beat, clubbed and kicked him as if he had purposely tried to escape and deserved great punishment for deliberate wrong doing. When he was down on the ground, they walked on his body even daring to step on his face while they laughed and carried on, shouting vile insults. [38] The bailiffs were extremely cruel to Our Lord with the ever present hope of gaining favor with the six powerful agents who approved of their every vile deed.

When they left the garden they turned north onto the low Bethany Road. Traveling for a short distance they turned toward the city to cross a bridge over the Kidron. Our Lord was smashed to the ground twice by actions of the bailiffs even before they reached the bridge. Often times when he fell they yanked him up by his hair.

The agents who remained close to Our Lord constantly unleashed their fury by demeaning and blaspheming him with vile comments against him and his doctrines. They never stopped slapping, punching, kicking and beating him with clubs and staves [39] and often jabbed him with pointed objects. They spit on him so often that his face was loaded with slimy dripping spittle. He had only been their captive for a few minutes and already his treatment was inhumane without compare.

They approached the bridge which was quite long as it not only crossed over the Kidron but part of the valley itself. They entered the bridge and as the neared the halfway point, they unleashed such a vicious barrage of blows on Our Lord and beat him so severely that he was forced over the rail and fell into the brook below. He landed on his knees and face and would have most certainly been killed if he had not put out his hands to break his fall, even though his hands were still securely tied behind his back. [40]

---

[38] This sort of treatment was done almost exclusively by the four bailiffs and the six agents. The soldiers did not take part in this senseless treatment.

[39] A stave is a long rod or staff about one and one fourth inches in diameter which can be used as a walking staff or to defend oneself against an enemy. You can deliver a nasty blow to "stave off an enemy."

[40] Our Lord resulted to a miracle to save himself from certain death as it was not yet the time or the manner in which he should die.

They sneered and laughed at him from above and in a contemptible manner suggested to him that he quench his thirst while he was down there. Being ravaged with violent thirst from blood sweating and ill treatment and to fulfill scripture [41] he did precisely as they suggested. While partially immersed in the Kidron, he drank.

The bailiffs tugged on the ropes but they couldn't pull him out on the city side because of a retaining wall so they turned around and dragged him back to the start of the bridge and forced him to cross over it a second time. All the ill treatment resumed immediately. His long woolen garments were drenched causing them to cling to his legs making it even more difficult for him to walk than before. Reaching the end of the bridge he stumbled on the edges of his own garments and fell hard to the ground. They dragged him to his feet by his hair and whipped him with the ends of the ropes. They roughly stuffed the ends of his garment into the leather belt so he wouldn't trip and cause any further delays. They continued their cowardly abuse from which they drew great delight.

On the city side of the Kidron they forced him along a rough road which was strewn with stones, fragmented rock, thorns and thistles. Our Lord was barefoot and his feet were cut, bruised and bleeding. Staying ever close to him the six agents jabbed and hit him constantly while the bailiffs jerked at the ropes and whipped him with the ends of them.

Seeing that his feet were torn and bloody one of the agents used it as an occasion to scorn him by saying that his precursor John the Baptist did not prepare a very good path for him while another chimed in that neither do the words of the Prophet Malachi, behold I send my Angel before you to prepare the way apply now. Every statement uttered by these agents incited the bailiffs to ever greater abuse which met with ever greater approval and favor.

During Our Lord's suffering, his Blessed Mother shared in all his torments right along with him. In addition she prayed

---

[41] "He shall drink from the brook by the wayside; therefore he shall lift up his head." Psalm 110.

along with the women in her company and the Angels of her guard, ever praising, adoring and confessing the Infinite God and the adorable humanity of her Divine Son. The more his enemies brutalized and irreverenced him the more they offered praise and adoration to compensate for their unholy actions. In this manner they not only saved his enemies from Divine punishment but even obtained blessings from Divine clemency for them.

During all this time, when Satan had been urging on the bailiffs and the agents of the High Priest he was closely observing every action and reaction of Our Lord. He was putting Our Lord's patience to the test in a most severe manner to see if he was only a man or more than a man. Not knowing the answer wounded his wicked pride. Observing the serene majesty of his patience and meekness without getting upset with all the injuries and suffering drove Satan to such a rage that he attempted to take the ropes from the bailiffs so he and his cohorts could yank them more violently than his wicked human allies and maybe cause Our Lord to lose his patience.

The Blessed Virgin, fully observing these actions of Satan, used her power as Sovereign Queen and issued a command to Satan not to interfere. All his power left him at once and he was unable to put his plan into practice. He was, however, given permission to allow his demons to incite his captors because as human beings they were free to make a choice to carry out their temptations or to refuse to do so. He used this permission to its fullest effect.

Satan made comment to his fellow demons saying; "what kind of man is this now born into the world who by his patience and his works so torments and annihilates us. None ever maintained such calmness and long suffering in tribulation since the time of Adam until now. Never have we found among mortals such humility and meekness. How can we rest when we see in the world such a rare and powerful example drawing others after him? If this is the Messiah he will certainly open Heaven and close up the highway by which we have so far led men into eternal torments. We shall be vanquished and all our plans frustrated. Even if he is but a mere man I cannot permit such an example for the rest of mankind. Haste then ministers of my exacted power. Let us persecute him through his human foes who obedient to my sway have conceived of me some of our furious envy." [42]

Our Lord submitted meekly to all the insults, blasphemies, blows and inhuman outrages without a harsh word or even a mild complaint. He did not open his mouth, attempt to escape or return insult for injury. He went meekly as a lamb being led to green pastures. He hid his Divine power with which he could have immediately crushed his enemies by an act of his will. Instead, he prayed.

As the arresting band came within site of the city gate which led into the village of Ophel just west of the Temple area, they noticed several persons in the distance observing their actions. These were Disciples who had come together after they had been informed that Our Lord had been arrested. Seeing them made the six agents fearful of a rescue attempt and they sent a messenger to the gate for reinforcements.

A group of about fifty soldiers were quickly assembled from the three hundred who lined the streets and went out to meet the arresting band. They shouted loudly as they approached not only to announce their arrival but also to congratulate their buddies on the success of their mission. There was momentary confusion as the two bands met and Malchus and some of the other soldiers who had fallen to the ground in the garden used this temporary disorder to defect and return to Mount Olivet in search of the Apostles as they had been completely overwhelmed by what had happened to them in the garden. They were changed men. [43]

As the Disciples watching from a distance saw the two bands of soldiers merge, they dispersed in different directions and left the area.

At about this same time, the Blessed Virgin, having left the Cenacle in the company of some of the women, Lazarus, John Mark and the son of Simon, came into the Kidron Valley. They watched the soldiers celebrate the capture of her Son and

---

[42] Quote from the Mystical city of God by Mary of Agreda.
[43] About ten in all.

she was filled with grief. She was still suffering the same torments in her body as he was and the effects were beginning to show as she became weak. Her companions decided that it was best to return her to the Cenacle as soon as they could.

In the village of Ophel the residents were beginning to stir as they were awakened by the noise of the soldiers and were beginning to leave their houses and spill out into the streets. They were mostly laborers, stone masons and low paid Temple workers. Both Our Lord and his doctrines were well known to them as he had preached to and cured many of their number. They asked the soldiers lining the streets what all the commotion was about but the soldiers pushed them back and ordered them to return to their homes. The people persisted and demanded to know what was going on at this late hour of the night. Finally the soldiers told them that they had arrested Jesus of Nazareth, their false Prophet and that he was going to be tried and crucified.

The people were at first shocked and filled with disbelief. They began discussing among themselves all that he had done for them and told one another of their own cures or conversions. They cried out loud with all their complaints and kneeled in the streets to implore Heaven to intervene.

The soldiers hit them and pushed them aside in an attempt to clear the street, while remarking among themselves that no more proof was needed that he incites rebellion as these people were proving it. Seeing the reaction of the crowd, the soldiers backed off somewhat and modified their treatment of the people for fear of an all out insurrection. They only pushed the crowd back from the area in which they would have to bring Our Lord through.

As the arresting band and their reinforcements reached the gate at Ophel Our Lord fell to the ground and appeared unable to go on for they had never let up on their abuse for even a second. One soldier who was moved by pity for Our Lord admonished the rest to open up their eyes and see that the man was already completely exhausted and could barely support himself under the weight of his heavy chains. He firmly advised them that if they wished to arrive at the residence of the High Priest with him still alive they had better loosen the bindings on his hands so that he could give himself a little protection when he falls. They stopped for a moment and heeding the soldiers advice, loosened the bonds on his hands.

Another soldier seeing a water fountain close by brought Our Lord some water to drink. The Savior thanked him and spoke to him of fountains of living water of which those who believed in him should drink. [44]

This infuriated the six agents who heaped blasphemies and insults upon him anew and treated him with even more contempt.

Once again they began to move and as they passed through the gate into the village of Ophel cries of grief and sympathy went up from the excited crowd who owed him so much. Many cries of "release him to us", were heard from among the people of Ophel. They were grief stricken at the sight of him and they looked upon the Lord with horror. He was pale, disfigured and sorely wounded. His hair was a mess and his clothing was wet and filthy. The crowds pressed forward and screamed at the soldiers to give him up and the soldiers had their hands full trying to keep them at bay.

The bailiffs were dragging and whipping Our Lord to get him to hurry past the crowd. He was beaten and struck without mercy and in this manner was hurried through the crowd and conducted to the palace of the former High Priest Annas.

Peter and John had been following the procession at a distance and quickly made their way to the Palace of the High Priest Annas who John knew well. They went directly to some servants with whom John was familiar and expressed their desire to get in to see the trial. These same servants had just been ordered to go into the city and summon the elders and assembly members to convene the Sanhedrin. They wanted to help the two Apostles but were afraid that it would be very difficult to get them in. They solved the problem by giving them cloaks like they themselves wore and had them assist in carrying messages so they would blend in. Then, they concluded, after the messages

---

[44] These two soldiers, enlightened by grace for their good deeds would later become believers.

were delivered they could enter the tribunal without being recognized.

The soldiers had disappeared in the direction of Mount Zion, dragging Our Lord with them but the people of Ophel were still milling around in the streets when the Blessed Virgin entered the gate with her companions. They expressed their profound grief to the Holy Mother and wept openly, venting to her their overwhelming sorrow.

The Holy Mother was speechless with grief and was suffering terribly by the time they reached the Cenacle. About that time John arrived dressed in the cloak of one of the High Priests messengers. He told her all that had taken place since they had gone forth from the supper room that night. Although she had seen, heard and felt in her own body and soul all that had happened she listened intently to all the Apostle had to say.

As soon as John finished his story he went out to rejoin Peter who was in the process of informing Joseph of Arimathea, Nicodemus and other well intentioned assembly members. The Apostles related to them all that was going on as they knew they would not be summoned by anyone else. The Pharisees had not intended to summon any of the council members who might be favorable to Our Lord.

Most of Jerusalem had now been awakened by all the commotion and had learned of the arrest. Many locked themselves in their homes fearing there was going to be a riot.

The Romans had not taken part in any of these events. They had no understanding of what the city was so excited about. Observing the entire city come to life at this hour of the night was reason enough for them to be concerned. All sentries were doubled and the entire Cohort of one thousand men were awakened and placed on full alert. They kept a strict outlook on the city from the towers of the Fortress Antonio. The Governor, Pontius Pilate, had received a message from the High Priest giving his reason for stationing Temple Guards around the city and outside the walls. Pilate was not very trusting of their actions as there was a great deal of bad feelings between the Romans and the Jews. He was very suspicious of their intentions. [45]

As the Pharisees, elders and assembly members made their way through the streets they took great pains to avoid the Roman sentries so they would not have to answer any questions. At this point in time they did not want the Romans involved so they could attend to their foul affair without interference.

Most of the Apostles were terror stricken. They wandered back and forth in the valleys that surrounded Jerusalem. They sometimes hid themselves in caves outside the city meeting one another on occasion and discussing the events but if they heard the slightest sound they separated immediately. Some had climbed to the top of Mount Olivet to follow the procession of torches which were now appearing all over the city. They watched intently as most of the torches congregated on Mount Zion in the areas of the High Priest's residence.

At times they went back into the Kidron Valley or even sneaked into the city to see if they could get a little news as to what was happening to their Master. They retreated in fear at every sound anywhere near them or if they thought they saw some movement in the shadows. All of them reflected on the suffering of his Mother and how they wished it were possible for them to console her in this hour.

From the recesses of the Cenacle Our Holy Mother witnessed and suffered all; not only because of the terrible sufferings of her Holy Son but also because of the sufferings the Apostles were going through. She knew their trials, temptations, thoughts and resolves. She knew where each one was and what he was doing at any given time. She did not allow herself to harbor any ill feelings or indignation against the Apostles or would she ever in the future bring up the subject of their disloyalty. Instead she was the one responsible for restoring them to a better frame of mind. She loved them dearly.

---

[45] During the course of this night, Pilate would not be getting much sleep but would be wandering about issuing orders in response to the reports coming from his sentries. His wife would sleep but would be greatly disturbed by terrible dreams.

She prayed earnestly for them; O you simple sheep chosen by the Lord, do you forsake your most loving pastor who cares for you and feeds you on the pastures of eternal life? Why, being Disciples of such a truthful doctrine, do you leave your benefactor and Master? How can you forget the sweet and loving conversations which so attracted your hearts? Why do you listen to the master of lies and follow the ravenous wolf who seeks your ruin? O most patient and sweetest Lord, how meek, lovable and kind does the love of men make you? Extend your gentle love to this little flock which is now troubled and dispersed by the fury of the serpent. Do not deliver over to the beasts those souls who have confessed your name. Great hopes have you set in those whom you have chosen as your servants and through whom you have already accomplished great things. Let such graces not be in vain or reject those you have freely chosen for the foundations of your church. Let not Satan glory in having beneath your very eyes, vanquished the best of your family and household. My Son and Lord look upon your Disciples John and Peter and James so much favored by your love and good will. Turn an eye of clemency also upon the rest. Crush the pride of the dragon which now pursues them with implacable fury." [46]

The desertion of the Apostles was a great source of sorrow for Our Lady. She knew that they were confused and afraid and would not be thinking about being assaulted by the powers of darkness even though they had been admonished several times to "watch and pray" and that this would leave them vulnerable to the furious attacks of Satan and his demons. She prayed with great fervor to her Divine Son for the grace to assist them in their trials and to obtain his pardon for them. She pleaded that they be given the grace to persevere in faith and for them to return to grace and devotion to her Son and Lord.

At this particular time, the darkest of hours, the Blessed Virgin Mary constituted the entire church. Contained in her was the entire deposit of faith, hope, love, complete worship and adoration preserved, not only for herself but for the Apostles and the whole human race. She alone could make up for what was

---

[46] Quote from the Mystical city of God by Mary of Agreda.

lacking in the rest of humanity. She made continual acts of faith, hope and love to her suffering Son and adored him with loving songs of praise in spite of her bitter sorrow and suffering. Using all the faculties at her disposal she interceded for all humanity.

Enclosed in the tabernacle of her bosom was the body, blood, soul and Divinity of her Divine Son in the Blessed Sacrament which she had received hours earlier at the first ever Mass. At this moment in time and until the church will be born at Pentecost she is the incorruptible Ark containing the evangelical law and Holy Sacrifice.

Chapter III
The Religious Trials

Reaching the compound of the High Priests, they brought Our Lord to the house of Annas the former High Priest [47] and father in law of Joseph Ciaphas, the current High Priest. Annas was not quite yet ready to receive Our Lord so they tied him to a tree in the courtyard. [48] Annas was completely beside himself at the thought of Our Lord finally being brought before his tribunal. He was the head of a tribunal which was charged with investigating all cases of blasphemy. He had been impatiently awaiting Our Lord's appearance ever since he had heard of his capture in the garden. It was mainly Annas who had made all the arrangements with Judas for his betrayal and apprehension. It was he who was doing most of the bribing and assembling of false witnesses. In his glee, he could not hide his hatred and envy of Our Lord.

It was about midnight when the guards untied Our Lord from the tree and dragged him into the great hall within the house of Annas. The High Priest was seated on an elevated platform surrounded by many councilors. Seated next to Annas, but unknown to him, was Satan and many of his evil spirits. [49]Annas was well along in years and was very well versed in Jewish Law and politics. He was famous for being shrewd, cunning and of a great intellect.

The Bailiffs presented Our Lord to the tribunal just as he was, tied and chained like a wild animal.

---

[47] Annas had been High Priest from AD 6 to AD15 when the Romans deposed him and replaced him in violation of Jewish Law. Many considered him to still be the rightful High Priest.

[48] There is still an olive tree growing on that very spot in Jerusalem where the olive tree stood that they tied him to.

[49] In total contrast Our Lord was surrounded by adoring Angels who honored him for his judgments and wisdom in allowing himself to be presented as a criminal and sinner.

One of the bailiffs addressed Annas saying; "At last we bring here this wicked man who by his sorcery and evil deeds has disturbed all Jerusalem and Judea. This time his magic has not allowed him to escape us." [50]

The large hall was filled to capacity with tribunal members, temple guards, household servants, false witnesses and a number of the mob of people who had gained admittance to see what was going to happen. Judas had gained entry with the arresting band and was allowed to witness the proceedings.

Our Lord appeared ragged and exhausted from his agony in the garden and all the mistreatment he had endured at the hands of his captors. His hands were still cuffed and bound with ropes and chains [51] and his clothing was wet and soiled with mud, manure, spit and blood. In all patience and humility he stood before the tribunal, head bowed and silent. They finally untied his hands.

Annas was frail looking and very thin. He was old, had a scraggly beard and no sense of humor. With great arrogance and scorn apparent in his voice he tried to pretend that he knew nothing at all about Our Lord's capture and was really surprised to learn that the prisoner before him was Jesus of Nazareth.

Just before Annas was about to speak Our Lord offered to his Eternal Father all the humiliation of being presented as a criminal before the former High Priest and being questioned as a liar and teacher of false doctrine.

With all the contempt he could muster, Annas addressed Our Lord saying; "Is it possible that you are Jesus of Nazareth? Where are you're Disciples; you're numerous followers? Where is your kingdom? I fear affairs did not turn out as you expected. The authorities, I presume, discovered that it was quite time to put a stop to your conduct, disrespectful as it was to God and his Priests and to such violations of the Sabbath. What Disciples do you have now? Where have they all gone? You are silent? Speak

---

[50] Quote from the Mystical city of God by Mary of Agreda.

[51] It was customary for the Jews to present a prisoner tied and changed who was in their opinion deserving of a death penalty. However, in this case, no charges had even been filed yet.

out, you seducer! Speak out, you inciter of rebellion! Did you not eat the Paschal Lamb in an unlawful manner, at an improper time and in an unlawful place? Do you not desire to introduce new doctrines? Who gave you the right to preach? Where did you study? What are the tenets of your religion?"

Our Lord understands only too well that Annas is not the official judge in this matter and that he is not God's delegate. Ciaphas is! Annas is only wasting valuable time in the work of redemption and is adding to his own innumerable sins. To prevent both, the merciful heart of Our Lord will end this delay with a short terse response.

He raised his weary head and said to Annas; "I have spoken openly to the world. I have always taught in the Synagogues and in the Temple where all the Jews go. In secret, I have spoken nothing. Why ask me? Ask those who have heard what I have spoken to them. They know what I have said."

Annas became flushed with anger at this answer. This so called learned man of the law, this self proclaimed judge with no legal authority is shown to be ignorant of his own duties. Our Lord's answer to him is a severe rebuke. [52]

One of the bailiffs who was standing close by saw the indignation of the High Priest and struck Our Lord in the face with an iron gauntlet [53] causing him to stagger, saying at the same time; "Is that how you answer the High Priest?" Then more bailiffs rebuked him and struck him until he fell to the floor with blood oozing from his battered face.

---

[52] This answer contains many rebukes to Annas. 1. Our Lord is telling him that he has said nothing in secret that he has not said in public. By contrast, Annas had done everything to effect his arrest in secret. 2. He said, why ask me? The force and truthfulness of his teachings, by their own excellence should have been recognized by him as coming from God. 3. Under Mosaic Law, you may not bind, chain and torture someone as already guilty and then afterwards hold a hearing to find evidence for an accusation. Witnesses should have been ready to testify to the truthful facts, hence, why ask me? 4. Concerning the Apostles, he said nothing. The rebuke was silent.

[53] A heavy leather glove covered with metal plates to protect the hand during combat.

Laughter, bitter insults and scornful words could be heard throughout the large hall. The bailiffs roughly dragged Our Lord to his feet by his hair. Our Lord accepted this horrible treatment and prayed especially for the one who first struck him. He turned to that bailiff and said meekly and calmly; "If I have spoken evil, give testimony of evil; but if I have spoken rightly, why do you strike me?" The bailiff did not reply.

With this humble reply of Our Lord the evil intent of the High Priest stood shamefully exposed to all; but neither the reprimand or the illegality of these proceedings served to deter this wicked council from its unholy course. Seeing the calm demeanor of Our Lord and hearing his public reprimand enraged Annas even more. He demanded that the witnesses come forth with their accusations.

The witnesses came forward and all began to speak at the same time airing many unfounded and distorted accusations such as; "He calls himself King and says that God is his Father. He said that the Pharisees are an adulterous generation. He causes insurrections among the people and cures the sick with the Devil's help on the Sabbath day. The people in the village of Ophel call him Savior and Prophet and he allows himself to be called the Son of God. He claims to be sent by God and predicts the destruction of Jerusalem. He doesn't fast and he eats his meals with sinners, pagans, tax collectors and even associates with shady women. He seduces people by using words that have more than one meaning." Many of them insulted, mocked and made fun of Our Lord as they spoke. The bailiffs often hit him saying; "Speak! Why don't you answer?"

As the witnesses droned on, Annas and some of his councilors injected their own questions; "Is this your doctrine then? What can you answer to this? Are you the son of a carpenter or are you Elias who was carried up to Heaven in a fiery chariot of whom it is said that he is still living? We are told that you can make yourself invisible at will. Maybe you are the Prophet Malachi whose words you so often quote, an imposter like you could not have a better opportunity of deceiving the people then by passing yourself off as a Prophet. Tell us to what order of kings to you belong? Are you greater than Solomon as you pretend to be? Do you really expect to be believed?"

"Well be at peace," Annas sneered, "I will no longer refuse you the title and the scepter which is justly due you." [54]

Annas ordered that a sheet of parchment [55] be given to him on which he wrote down all the accusations that he though Ciaphas should consider. He rolled it up, stuffed it into a hollow tube, fastened it to the top of a reed and gave the reed to Our Lord to carry. With an air of contempt he told Our Lord to behold the scepter of his kingdom as it contained the titles and list of honors to which he was entitled and his right to the throne.[56] He told him that the High Priest would acknowledge his regal dignity and give him his just desserts.

He then ordered his hands to be retied and instructed the bailiffs to take him to the High Priest Ciaphas. His hands were retied across his chest in such a way as to allow him to carry the make shift scepter and parchment which contained the accusations made by Annas. [57]

The soldiers and bailiffs led Our Lord back out into the courtyard and turned south toward the house of Ciaphas. [58] The assembled mobs in the courtyards began shouting, hissing and reviling Our Lord as the guards escorted him through their midst. Many struck him when he came near enough and the guards and bailiffs did nothing to protect him.

They crossed the outer courtyard which was in front of the house of Annas and passed through a gate into an inner courtyard which led to the house of Ciaphas. The palace of

---

[54] Some quotes of this trial are from the Mystical city of God by Mary of Agreda, The Dolorous passion of Our Lord Jesus Christ by Anne Catherine Emmerich in conjunction with the Gospels.

[55] Writing material made out of sheep or goat skin.

[56] Even without realizing it the enemies of Our Lord keep uttering the truth about him. The title and the scepter are his just due, even though they only intend to mock him.

[57] In accordance with the law, the hands of Our Lord were untied during the brief hearing. It was a meaningless gesture in this case. It was to show that he had full freedom to defend himself.

[58] The houses of Annas and Ciaphas faced each other across a large courtyard about one hundred yards in length.

Ciaphas was a large rectangular building with a large open vestibule to its front. The vestibule roof was supported by large columns and in the middle of the floor there was a fire pit whose chimney extended through the vestibule roof. Many servants and temple guards were warming themselves around the fire pit.

Our Lord was dragged through the vestibule, then up a flight of steps and into a large room where the Sanhedrin met. [59] The council seats were on a raised platform and arranged in the form of a half circle. The throne of the High Priest was in the middle of them and situated a little higher than the rest. Most of the council members were already seated around Ciaphas but a few were still being rounded up. There were so many torches and lanterns that the room was lit as bright as day.

As soon as Our Lord appeared in the council chamber cuffed, chained and being pulled like a dog on a leash, he was met with laughter and ridicule by the High Priest and his council. What a joy it was for them to see him humbled in such a manner, helpless and completely within their power.

Our Blessed Lord offered this humiliating experience to his Heavenly Father to compensate for the malicious sins of these very persecutors. He made excuses for them because they exercised such colossal ignorance.

Suffering in complete unison with her Divine Son, the Holy Mother, witnessing all from the Cenacle, offered her prayers for her enemies and those of her Son. The Eternal Father was well pleased with the actions of both Son and Mother as meekness; patience and love were defeating sin.

On the other hand, the demons were confused and furious at not being able to penetrate the invincible patience and meekness of Our Lord. He never complained. He never asked for relief from his sufferings. Satan was not sure on just how to approach this situation because this type of reaction to immense suffering was not normal among weak human mortals. He increased his efforts to irritate the enemies of Our Lord so they

---

[59] Since the Romans had taken away the right to level the death penalty from the Jewish Nation, they no longer met in the tribunal room in the great Temple but in the house of Ciaphas, away from Roman eyes.

would use even greater cruelty in his treatment. Sadly, they were only too eager to comply.

Peter and John had made their way into the outer courtyard still dressed as messengers, just before they had led Our Lord through. They had gained entrance into the inner courtyard because of the way they were dressed. They had made their way through the mob, hoping to get into the courtroom in the house of Ciaphas. John managed to get in with the help of a house servant whom he knew but the door was closed just as Peter was about to enter, leaving him in the vestibule. Peter and John both pleaded with the door keeper to let Peter in but she steadfastly refused both of them. While they were still trying to convince the door keeper, Joseph of Arimathea and Nicodemus arrived and took Peter in with them. Peter and John stood in a place where they could see the council and hear the proceedings without being too conspicuous. It was at this time that they returned the messenger cloaks to the servant who let them use them.

When Our Lord was led through he had glanced at Peter and John with his eyes but did not turn his head so as not to give them away. He was pulled and shoved to the area where the council was assembled. He was made to stand in front of Ciaphas in the presence of the ever attending bailiffs. Many public officials took their place to either side of Our Lord and the Temple Guards formed a corridor from the base of the platform to the vestibule door to maintain order. [60]

The High Priest, seething with contempt and hatred, made no attempt to hide his feelings. He sat arrogantly on his throne in the company of Satan and his demons who had come from the

---

[60] The Sanhedrin consisted of seventy one members. The reigning High Priest was the head of the court. The court was made up of the elders of Jerusalem's most influential families, Chief Priests, (including those who had once been High Priest, mostly the sons of Annas) and scribes who were experts on the laws of Moses. (Lawyers) Many council members belonged to one of the two current political parties, the Sadducees or the Pharisees. The council could conduct trials of both civil and religious affairs without consulting the Romans as long as capital punishment was not an issue.

house of Annas to assist him. He wore a long red mantle [61] which was embroidered with flowers and trimmed in gold. It was fastened at his chest and shoulders with gold clasps. His head piece very much resembled the miter of a Bishop.

Ciaphas had been waiting impatiently for Our Lord to arrive. He had made several trips to the vestibule door in the past hour to see if he was coming and now, finally, here he stood before him.

When all were settled before the High Priest, Ciaphas called for silence. [62] Then he addressed Our Lord in a loud voice saying; "You are come at last, you enemy of God; you blasphemer who disturbed the peace of this holy night." He came forward, grabbed the tube from Our Lord and ordered his hands untied. He then returned to his throne and opened and read the parchment. When he was through he heaped many insults and much verbal abuse on Our Lord and asked him many rapid fire questions. Our Lord did not answer or even look at him. The bailiffs hit him many times, screaming at him to answer.

Ciaphas filled with more rage then even Annas had exhibited, kept on asking question after question but still Our Lord would not raise his head or look at him. The bailiffs punched him repeatedly in an effort to make him speak.

Seeing that he was getting nowhere, Ciaphas called for the witnesses to be heard. The first to testify were the so called high class witnesses, namely Pharisees, Sadducees and scribes from all over the country who were in Jerusalem for the festival. Their hatred and envy showed with every false and misrepresented accusation. All they could testify to was the same old tired nonsense, such as; "that he cured the sick and cast out demons with the help of demons. That he violated the Sabbath and incited the people to rebel. That he called the Pharisees a race of viper and adulterers. That he predicted the destruction of

---

[61] A long sleeveless cape which covered the shoulders and hung down to the ankles.

[62] Joseph Ciaphas was High Priest from AD 18 when he was installed by the Romans, to AD 36 when he was deposed by the Romans. He was the son in law of Annas.

Jerusalem and associated with tax collectors and sinners. They accused him of claiming to be a king, prophet and Son of God. They said he constantly talked about his kingdom and even dared to say that he was the bread of life and that if you did not eat his flesh and drink his blood you would not have eternal life.

Accusation followed accusation but none of the witnesses could agree. They not only contradicted each other but even began to argue among themselves. No facts or reliable proof was presented by any of them and nothing could be proven in compliance with Mosaic Law.

Ciaphas silenced the witnesses and returned to questioning Our Lord himself. He asked questions and Our Lord made no answer. And the bailiffs hit him. This went on for several minutes, through several questions and several punches. [63]

Some of the witnesses came forth and accused Our Lord of being illegitimate. They were immediately contradicted by others who knew that his Mother had been raised as one of the Temple Virgins and that she had been properly wed to a good and holy man. Others came forward and testified that Our Lord and his Disciples never offered sacrifice in the Temple and accused him many times of being a sorcerer.

Ciaphas remarked many times in the course of these testimonies that the confusion of the witnesses was caused by witchcraft. The more these witnesses contradicted each other the more annoyed the High Priest became. No one had said any one thing that carried with it one shred of proof of any wrong doing.

More witnesses came up and accused our Lord of having eaten the Paschal Lamb the day before it was allowed by law and that he and his Disciples had altered the holy rite. Not only that but they had eaten it in a house owned by two of their very own council members, Joseph of Arimathea and Nicodemus.

---

[63] Keep in mind the fact that Our Lord is not yet officially charged with any crime. He is only being questioned. Mosaic Law is not only being broken by these proceedings; it is being buried. Everything so far is illegal. Our Lord is being systematically tortured to give the kind of answers they want to hear.

The questioning then turned to the two Pharisees to explain why they had allowed such a thing to take place in a building owned by them. They came forward and produced ancient documents that showed that for a long period of time now the Galilean's have had permission under the law to eat the Paschal Lamb a day earlier than the rest of the nation because if all the people of Israel had to eat it on the same day there would not be enough time to complete the sacrifice before the onset of the Sabbath as was also prescribed by law. Further more, they stated, that the entire ceremony conducted in their house was in full compliance with the law and that many people belonging to the Temple had been present.

After this testimony the witnesses became more confused than ever and the enemies of Our Lord even more enraged at having been presented with irrefutable proof that no wrong doing had taken place. Most of the council was furious with the two Pharisees for showing that the council had conducted the entire hurried affair in response to their hatred and envy and without proper preparation and sound evidence. There were no solid truthful witnesses as required and Our Lord was not getting due process of law. Even though they were completely upset by the two Pharisees they could not refute their defense. In any event, the council still allowed the false witnesses to prattle on in their ridiculous manner and continued to ask questions as if they actually had something of value to contribute to the proceedings.

Two more witnesses addressed the assembly and voiced a completely misunderstood version of something they had heard Our Lord say in the Temple saying; "This man said, I will destroy this temple made with hands and in three days I will build another not made with hands." Even though they testified as supposed experts neither one could agree on exactly what he had said or what it meant and began to argue among themselves in front of the whole assembly.

The confusion of the witnesses and the horrible treatment Our Lord was suffering with unheard of patience was beginning to make an impression on many of the council members to such an extent that they were beginning to have second thoughts. Some of them began to react unfavorably to many of the accusations as they found it difficult to drown out the voice of their conscience.

Ten of the Temple Guards, overcome by their feelings no longer found it possible to take part in these proceedings and turned away and started out of the courtroom. [64] As they came to the place where Peter and John were standing they stopped and said to them; "The silence of Jesus of Nazareth in the midst of such cruel treatment is superhuman. It could melt a heart of iron. The wonder is that the earth does not open up and swallow such reprobates as his accusers must be. Tell us where we must go." [65]

The two wary Apostles were not ready at this time to fully trust the intentions of these men and merely replied; "If truth calls you, follow it and all will come right of itself." They immediately left the hall and made their way out of the city to search for the remaining Apostles.

They soon learned that they were hiding in the caves of the Hinnom Valley south of Jerusalem. In a short time the guards found and entered the hiding place of the Apostles. At first they were seized with terror at having been discovered but the guards soon put them at rest and explained in full detail why they had come in search of them. They filled the Apostles in on all that was taking place and how terribly their Master was suffering.

In the courtroom, Ciaphas is fully aware that the situation is rapidly deteriorating and changing from his favor to Our Lord's. He becomes enraged to the point of loosing control as he leaps from his throne and screams at Our Lord; "have you no answer to these things they witness against you?" There was no answer and again Our Lord would not even look at him. Seeing that the High Priest was visibly seething with anger the bailiffs

---

[64] These ten who are now leaving are undoubtedly the remainder of the temple guards who fell in the garden of Gethsemane when Our Lord said, "I am He!"

[65] Quote from the Dolorous Passion of Our Lord Jesus Christ by Anne Catherine Emmerich. What an indictment of these proceedings! Just a short time ago these men had set out as part of an arresting band with full faith in the validity of their mission. Now they are so impressed by what has happened to them and by what they have seen that they wish to join the followers of the man they arrested. They have just turned their backs to the High Priest and placed themselves into the hands of the Apostles.

seized Our Lord by his hair, pulled his head back forcing him to raise it and then punched him repeatedly in the face in an attempt to make him answer. Even though his head was raised, Our Lord kept his glance downward and still would not look at or answer the High Priest.

Satan, at this point, was inciting the High Priest to badger Our Lord in an attempt to irritate him into giving some answer so that he could get some indication as to whether or not he was dealing with God or a mere man. He stirred up Ciaphas to a fever pitch then planted in his mind the idea to adjure him to tell if he was The Christ.

Ciaphas raised his hands and demanded in a voice filled with anger; "I adjure you by the living God that you tell us if you are The Christ; The Messiah; The Son of the Living God." [66] Complete silence came over the entire chamber as everyone strained to hear the reply should one be given. All eyes and attention were focused on Our Divine Lord as there was a long pause and a deafening silence. [67]Then Our Lord raised his head and looking Ciaphas directly in the eyes, declared in a steady strong voice for the whole world to hear for all time and said; "You have said it! I AM! [68]

As Our Lord utters his Divine answer special graces are given to all within range of his voice. Not wishing the loss of any sinner, Our Lord now dispenses even more graces while at the same time saying; "never the less, I say to you, hereafter you will see the Son of Man sitting at the right hand of the power of God,

---

[66] There are four reasons why Our Lord is finally going to answer the High Priest now. First, out of reverence for the name of God by whom Ciaphas has commanded him to speak. Second, in humble obedience to the High Priest who has the right to ask this question by nature of his office. Third, In order to deprive his judges of all excuses on the day of their judgment. Fourth, as High Priest, Ciaphas, without even realizing it is given the privilege of proclaiming the truth concerning the Messiah who is now before him.

[67] Having heard himself adjured by the Living God, Our Lord first adored and gave reverence to the Divinity, then made ready to answer.

[68] He is confirming the statement of the High Priest, assuring him that; "you have said it correctly, I am He!"

coming on the clouds of Heaven. [69] As he was speaking these words, Our Lord was surrounded by a bright light. Demons and men reacted differently to these words of Our Lord.

Satan and his demons couldn't stand what they heard and were immediately thrown down into hell and pinned there by the sheer force of the truth of these words. They would not have returned again into the presence of Our Lord if the almighty had not permitted them to become confused once again. They were still unsure whether or not his words were true or if he had said them in an attempt to be set free by the council. In this state of confusion, they returned to the battlefield. [70] They burst forth from hell with renewed fury and took possession of many persons in the council chamber and took up positions very near others. [71]

The High Priest, urged on by Satan cut his garment with a knife and tore it in two from top to bottom and exclaimed in a loud voice; "He has blasphemed! What further need have we of witness? Behold now, you have heard the blasphemy! What do you think?" The cry echoed throughout the chamber; "He is guilty of death!" [72]

The Priests, scribes and elders came forward and spit in Our Lord's face. [73]They also struck and kicked him and plucked out gobs of hair and beard. Some repeatedly struck him on the

---

[69] He is warning Ciaphas in no uncertain terms that now they are sitting in judgment of him but the next time they meet he will be sitting in judgment of them and he will be all powerful, not meek and humble as now.

[70] The final victory over Satan and his cohorts was to be fully apparent from the cross, not here.

[71] Classic examples of demonic possession and obsession.

[72] All those who had desired his death were now liable to the same judgment themselves at the moment they pronounced it. (Deut. Xix) If a lying witness stand against a man accusing him of crimes when after diligent questioning they shall find that the false witnesses lied against his brother, they shall do to him as he meant to do to his brother. You shall not pity him but shall require life for life, eye for eye, tooth for tooth, hand for hand, foot for foot. Under Jewish Law they should have suffered the same fate they wished for Our Lord.

[73] It was common practice for judges to rise and spit in the face of a condemned criminal.

72

neck, a treatment reserved for the vilest of criminals. Urged on by satanic fury their treatment was above and beyond the understanding of normal human cruelty.

The High Priest then turned him over to the custody of the bailiffs advising that he was delivering the king into their hands and that they should render to the blasphemer the honors to which he is due. The council members then left the courtroom chamber and assembled in another large room directly to the rear of the chamber in another part of the house of Ciaphas.

John was sick at heart. His thoughts went out to Our Lord's Holy Mother to whom he was deeply devoted. He was afraid that some unthinking soul might give her the news of her Son's condemnation in a harsh manner. He did not yet know that she was aware of all that was going on and suffering the same pains. He set out as quick as he could for the Cenacle to give an account of the courts proceedings.

Peter was overcome with sorrow and fatigue. Leaving the chamber he went out into the vestibule and began warming him self at the fire pit as the morning air was cold and damp. He couldn't bring himself to leave just yet as he needed to see what was to become of his beloved Master.

As soon as Ciaphas and the other council members had left the chamber the captors of Our Lord along with some of the mob that had congregated around him began to torment him with the cruelest of treatment. They were upset by the beautiful light which surrounded his face which continued to be present from the moment he had said; "I AM!" They blamed it on sorcery and put a dirty rag over his face so they wouldn't have to look at it.

They punched him repeatedly and said; "prophesy! Who was it that struck you?" Some of them made a crown of straw and bark and placed it on his head. They mocked him saying; "Behold the Son of David wearing the crown of his Father; a greater than Solomon is here! This is the king who is preparing a wedding feast for his Son." While they were mocking him they also struck him with fists and sticks while continually spitting on him. When they tired of this they replaced the mock crown with a crown of reeds, removed his own clothing and threw an old ragged cloak over his shoulders which barely reached down to his knees. They hung a long iron chain around his neck which extended down to his knees where there were two iron rings attached that contained spikes that ripped at his knees when they forced him to walk. They put a reed into his once again shackled hands and continually spit in his face. They rubbed animal manure in his hair, on his chest and all over the ragged cloak they had put on him. They used the dirty rag which they had placed over his face as a blindfold and hit him repeatedly saying; "prophesy to us O Christ. Who is it that struck you?" He never answered them once, offered no resistance and suffered all in humility while continuing to pray for them.

They were so proud of their actions that they dragged Our Lord into the adjoining room where the council members had gone so they could make sport of him for all the council members to see. They covered him with more manure and spit and mockingly exclaimed; "receive your regal prophetic unction." They mocked the baptismal ceremony by pouring a basin of filthy water over his head and shoulders, then pretended to anoint him with precious oil saying; "you have been baptized in the pool of Bethsaida."

Ciaphas and the council looked on with approval and delight as they made fun of baptism. Then the bailiffs paraded him before the council members who mocked him with affronts and abusive language.

The more they abused him the more he prayed for them. The interior acts of piety performed by Our Lord in the midst of all this inhuman treatment is way beyond the understanding of the human intellect. The Blessed Virgin was the only one who knew and understood what was taking place in the heart of her Divine Son. This enabled her to imitate him to the highest degree possible and to offer to the Eternal Father the same interior acts as her Son. By his prayers and offerings while suffering these hellish torments, Our Lord obtained many graces for those who were to come after him and put his teachings and doctrines into practice. By his own example he was teaching an imperfect world how to actually live the beatitudes he had taught them earlier. He was now, by his actions, establishing those very beatitudes as a rule or way of life.

He prayed for and blessed the poor in spirit who were to imitate him in this virtue saying; "blessed are you in being stripped of earthly goods; for by my passion and death I am to entail upon you the Heavenly Kingdom as a secure and certain possession of voluntary poverty." [74]

He prayed for and blessed the meek that were to put up with adversities and tribulations in imitation of what he was now doing. He was now meekly suffering every imaginable torment even though at any moment he had the Divine power to put an immediate end to it. They will in turn possess the land of the hearts of good will of men through the peacefulness of their speech and the sweetness of their virtue.

He prayed for and blessed those who would weep while they sowed in tears. For them he obtained the bread of understanding and life so that afterwards they may harvest the fruits of everlasting joy. Now, by way of his example, he was sowing the seeds of his doctrine and church in this valley of tears.

He prayed for and blessed those who were to hunger and thirst for justice, truth, grace and glory which he was now in the process of earning for them far beyond their greatest desires. By his suffering example, man was being reconciled with God, justice was being satisfied and the gates of Heaven were being flung wide open for those who wished to follow him in.

He prayed for and blessed those who would imitate his mercy and have pity on all those who would offend and persecute them. He would obtain for them the fullest measure of mercy from his Father.

He prayed for and blessed the pure of heart who in imitation of him will sacrifice the desires of their flesh to preserve the purity of their souls. For they will become like him by receiving him and in the end they will see God.

He prayed for and blessed the peaceful of heart that did not resist the evil minded and deal with them sincerely, without resorting to vengeance. By so doing they will imitate their Eternal Father and Our Lord will earn for them the right to be

---

[74] Quote from the Mystical City of God by Mary of Agreda.

called children of God. By suffering persecution for justice sake they will become blessed heirs to the Celestial Kingdom. .

This is the manner in which Our Lord occupied himself while being tortured non-stop. The Holy Mother witnessed all this and suffered all that he suffered while making the same petitions for his enemies in union with her Divine Son. All the blessings bestowed on the human race by Our Lord were given over to the charge of the Blessed Virgin Mary who was appointed to be their Mother, Helper and Protrectress. [75] In the name of all humanity the sweetest of Mothers composed hymns of praise and thanksgiving because her Divine Son had elevated her to such a high place in the order of grace.

Peter sat by the fire in the vestibule listening to the soldiers and servants discussing the events and what they themselves had done to his Lord. Some of those around him couldn't help but notice that he was not taking part in the conversation. After a short time, the woman who was the gate keeper at the house of Annas came up to the fire pit to warm herself. By the light of the fire she recognized Peter and said; "You were also with Jesus of Nazareth." Peter was shocked as all eyes turned to him. "Woman," he replied; "I do not know the man." He rose quickly, left the vestibule and went into the inner courtyard. After a moment a cock crowed somewhere off in the distance but Peter did not seem to notice. As he moved about in the courtyard another woman said to him and to her companions; "This man is one of them!" Then her companions demanded that Peter tell them if her words were true or not saying; "are you one of this mans Disciples?" This second question scared the Apostle more than the first and he swore to them that he did not know the man.

Satan was out to destroy Peter and it was at his prodding that the two women called attention to him. At the same time he tempted Peter to think about all the cruel things he would have to suffer if he was discovered. This aided in prompting Peter's denials.

---

[75] All graces will now be dispersed through her, the great Mediatrix of graces.

Peter hurried through the gate into the outer court in front of the house of Annas and tried to loose himself in the crowd as their were more people milling around in this court than the inner court. Many had climbed over the walls of this court to see if they could find out what was going on. There were even a few Disciples [76] in the crowd trying to find out what was happening to their Master. When they spotted Peter they went straight up to him and asked many questions. Peter was so afraid at being discovered at this point that he abruptly told them to go away as it was too dangerous for them to be there. They quickly returned to their caves in the Hinnom Valley.

Peter was in agony. He was scared out of his wits but could not bring himself to leave. The suspense was killing him and after about an hour of wandering about in the outer court he decided to return to the inner court. He was allowed to pass because the gate keeper remembered that he had been with Joseph and Nicodemus earlier in the evening. This time he did not go near the fire pit in the vestibule. Gradually he made his way to an outside door which led into the hall where Our Lord was being tormented. Even though he knew that he might be discovered again, love for his Master overcame his fear for the moment and he entered the hall. At that moment they were dragging Our Lord back and forth while they continued to mock, insult and mistreat him. Our Lord looked at Peter with a sorrowful and somewhat stern gaze which made Peter sick at heart but at that very moment he heard someone yell; "who is that man?" and he scrambled back into the courtyard.

Noticing that those who were in the vestibule were watching him, Peter went boldly up to the fire in the hopes that no one would suspect him of anything. He remained there for quite some time warming himself.

Inside the hall, the High Priest and many of the council members showed great pleasure at the show their servants were giving them but it was already past midnight and they still had a great deal to do in the morning. They issued orders to the bailiffs

---

[76] No Apostles.

to confine Our Lord in one of the prison cells beneath the house of Ciaphas which was reserved for the worst of criminals.

For quite awhile no one said a word to Peter. Then suddenly one of those around the fire said to him; "you are also one of his Disciples! You are a Galilean! Even your speech betrays you!" Peter started to leave the vestibule once again when the brother of Malchus [77] came up and said; "didn't I see you in the garden with him?" Peter was terror stricken at being discovered again and began to curse and swear that he did not know the man.

At that moment Our Lord was brought into the vestibule by his captors and witnessed Peter's denial. The look Our Lord gave to Peter pierced him to the depths of his soul. At that moment, somewhere in the hearing of all those in the vestibule a cock crowed for the second time. This time Peter took notice and remembered the words of his Master from the previous evening; "before the cock crows twice you will deny me three times."

From her room in the Cenacle the Holy Mother had witnessed all of Peter's denials and she was fully aware of all the circumstances which caused his denials, his natural fears and all the torments of Satan. She fell prostrated on the floor and interceded for Peter, appealing to all the merits her Divine Son was gaining for sinners.

As Our Lord looked upon his devastated Apostle he sent a holy light into his soul which made Peter aware of a gentle reproach from his beloved Master telling him to own up to his fault and to despise his sin. Peter was filled with remorse; his heart broken and he was suffering to the very depths of his immense grief. He immediately burst into tears and went into the outer court weeping most bitterly. He was no longer afraid to be recognized; he was ready to confess his faults for the entire world to hear.

The Blessed Virgin was ever united to her Divine Son throughout the entire passion. Eagerly desiring to be physically near him she asked John to take her to the place where he was suffering his torments. She set out with John and her female

---

[77] The soldier whose ear Peter had cut off in the garden of Gethsemane.

companions to the house of Ciaphas which was not far from the Cenacle. As they neared the house of Ciaphas they came across a group of men who were laboring under an open tent making a cross. They were not happy at having to toil through the night and made no attempt to conceal their anger but cursed and swore and made terrible oaths that penetrated the soul of this most Holy Mother. She prayed for these men as they blasphemed her Son while they prepared the instrument of his execution. [78]

They made their way into the outer courtyard and stopped at the gate to the inner courtyard. The Holy Mother desired with all her heart to see her Divine Son and to see the door open so that she could be near him. They waited for a while in silence when suddenly the door flew open and Peter rushed into their midst sobbing uncontrollably. Being suddenly thrust into the midst of the Holy Mother, John and all the holy women further deepened Peter's remorse and feelings of guilt. Our Lady approached Peter and said; "Simon, tell me I beg you, what has become of Jesus, my Son?" Peter was beside himself with grief and couldn't even look at her. The Holy Mother came closer and spoke in a trembling voice; "Simon, son of John. Why do you not answer me?" "Mother," stammered Peter; "O Mother, do not speak to me. Your Son is suffering more than words can express. Do not speak to me. They have condemned him to death and I have denied him three times." [79]John approached to ask some questions but Peter pulled away and ran out into the city. He did not stop running until he reached the Mount of Olives where he took refuge in a cave. [80]

The Mother of God was deeply distressed at the sorrow inflicted upon the heart of her Divine Son at hearing himself denied by the very same Apostle who was the first to recognize him as the Son of God. The denials of Peter caused Our Lord more pain than all the blows and insults given by his tormenters.

---

[78] Our Lord had not yet been taken before the Roman Governor but orders had been given to prepare a cross anyway.
[79] Quote from the Dolorous passion of Our Lord Jesus Christ by Anne Catherine Emmerich.
[80] To this very day this is know as the cockcrow cave.

He was willing to accept the pain and suffering inflicted by them as these were the instruments of atonement and redemption by which he was freeing the human race from its sins, but the denials of Peter were in terrible opposition to his charity and extremely repulsive to him filling him with immense feelings of sadness. She not only felt all the sufferings of the wounds and torments of her Son but also shared in his sadness as well and wept bitterly over the fall of Peter.

Still carrying within her breast her Divine Son in sacramental form, [81] she directed her praise, adoration and petitions to him until she saw that he would give to Peter all he needed to avoid despair and repent of his sins.

In the cave on Mount Olivet, Peter continued to weep bitterly over his sins. The Blessed Virgin sent one of the Angels of her guard to console him and to incite him to hope for forgiveness for his sins. The Angel was not allowed to appear to him because his sin had been so recently committed.

Our Lord was taken by his captors to a filthy cell beneath the house of Ciaphas which was well isolated from the rest of the house so that its horrible stench would not penetrate the living quarters and halls. No one ever cleaned it and it was loaded with human manure. Only the worst of criminals were kept here, especially those who were deemed to be unworthy of any human consideration. The cell only had one air vent which was so high up as to be out of reach and contained no windows at all.

As Our Lord entered the cell, he prayed that his Heavenly Father would accept all that he had suffered up to now and all that he was about to suffer in atonement not only for all his tormenters but for all who in future ages might have to suffer similar torments in his name. He prayed that they would be able to endure their sufferings without giving in to anger and impatience.

After Peter had burst through the door between the inner and outer courts it had been left open as many people were

---

[81] Our Lord remained in the tabernacle of his Holy Mother from the eve of the last supper until the Apostles began to offer Mass after Pentecost, fulfilling the promise; "I am with you always, even to the end of the world."

beginning to disperse and go to their homes. Our Blessed Lady requested John to bring her near to where her Son would be, so John took the entire party near to the door of the prison cells where Our Lord was confined. Even though through the grace of God she knew all that was taking place she desired to be near enough to hear his voice. [82]

Once inside the underground cell the bailiffs tied him to a large rock which stuck up out of the floor and was shaped like a natural column. It stood by itself in one corner of the filthy dungeon. They tied him to it in a stooping position in a manner that made it impossible to either sit or stand to get any relief. He was still clothed in the torn and dirty mantle and was still covered with spit and manure because they had never untied his hands and allowed him to put on his own clothes or to clean himself off. They left two of the bailiffs in the cell with him and went out and locked the door. The key was then put in the charge of one of the most evil minded of all the captors.

Satan still desired to know for certain who this man was and why his disgusting patience could not be overcome. He immediately began to work on the captor who had been given the key to go back into the dungeon with some of his companions to try and force Our Lord to prophesy or perform some outlandish stunt playing on their belief that he was some sort of a magician.

While these evil men were outside his cell discussing ways to torment Our Lord, several Angels from his Mother's guard came into his cell, prostrated themselves on the dirty floor and adored him. They displayed great reverence, worship and deep admiration for the immeasurable love which caused him to suffer so much abuse for the sake of his creatures. They sang to him songs and canticles which his own Mother had composed in his honor. When they had finished they begged him in the name

---

[82] John is apparently well known around the area of the High Priests homes. And by the servants, as he seems able to come and go as he pleases within these compounds. There are some references to the fact that he may have been related in some way to the High Priest Annas but no one states that for certain. It must have been common knowledge that he is an Apostle of Our Lord but no one challenges him or makes any attempt to arrest him throughout the passion.

of his Most Holy Mother that since he would not use his almighty powers to ease his sufferings that he allow them to untie him and release him from his painful position and then defend him from those whom Satan had incited and were now coming to torment him further.

He did not grant the Angels their wish to defend him saying; "ministering spirits of my Eternal Father, I do not wish to accept any alleviation of my sufferings at present. I desire to undergo these torments and affronts in order to satisfy fully my burning love for men and to leave my chosen friends this example for their imitation and consolation in their own sufferings and also in order that all men may properly judge the worth of the treasures of grace which I am gaining for them in great abundance through my pains. At the same time I wish to justify my cause so that on the day of my wrath all may know how justly the unrepentant sinner will be condemned for despising the most bitter sufferings by which I tried to save them. Tell my Mother to console herself in this tribulation since the day of rest and gladness will come. Let her accompany me now in my works and sufferings for men; for her affectionate compassion and all her actions afford me much pleasure and enjoyment." [83]

The Holy Angels left him and returned to his Mother and told her all that he had asked them to. She was already aware of what they had come to tell her and was already suffering in her own body the pains of this new cruelty caused by the way her Son was shackled to the pillar. [84]

A short time after the Angels left, the guards and servants entered the putrid filth of the cell to carry out their diabolical plan to inflict more torture. Once again they began a new round

---

[83] Quote from the Mystical city of God by Mary of Agreda.

[84] Our Lord suffered as God-man, the sole redeemer of the human race, the actual torments inflicted by these cruel men. His Holy Mother suffered as a creature and a faithful helper of her Divine Son by being allowed by Divine intervention to feel all the sufferings her Son was enduring. It was by her request which the Holy Trinity was pleased to allow. Without special help from the Eternal she would have died. In so doing she earned the title Co-redemptrix.

of beatings while covering him with more spit and mocking him as they went; heaping the vilest of insults upon him. They untied him from the pillar and made him stand in the middle of the cell where they once again blindfolded him with a filthy rag. Our Lord could hardly remain standing unaided as he was completely worn out from carrying the chains, beatings and many falls. The pain in his swollen mangled feet was unbearable and he fought to keep his balance.

They took turns tormenting him as they tried to get some sort of a response out of him but he continued to meekly allow all their indignities without the reaction they had hoped for. Incited by demons they became more an more cruel with the passing of each moment, punching, slapping and kicking him as if trying to out do each other in barbarity while asking him to prophesy as to who had done it. He endured their savagery with complete humility, meekness and patience while continually praying for them.

Satan was more upset than ever and not seeing any sign that he was losing patience flew into a fit of rage and incited the guards to remove all his clothing and sexually abuse him.

The Holy Mother, seeing what they were up to was moved to tears by great indignation. Now for the first time in the passion she uses her powers as the great Queen and petitions the Eternal Father not to allow the bodies of his tormenters to perform their natural functions in carrying out these unacceptable deeds which they were about to perform. Her prayer was answered immediately and some of the tormenters forgot right away what they had proposed to do. As others tried to strip his clothes off and abuse him their arms would not move until they changed their intentions. When they finally decided not to disrobe him and carry out their foul intentions their limbs began to function properly again. [85]

Our Blessed Lady then forbid the demons to follow Satan's intentions regarding this matter and ordered them to be silent so that they could no longer incite the tormenters to

---

[85] This was not intended as a punishment but only to prevent the foul deed.

attempt such things again, Due to her intercession Satan lost all his power in this particular matter. [86]

The demons, guards and servants were left free to practice their other torments and cruelties but not indecency. Divine wisdom had decided in advance that his Holy Mother would be the one to safeguard the innocence of her Son. [87]

Even though the tormenters had lost the use of their limbs and then regained them again it did nothing to soften their attitudes. They chalked it up to magic and continued to use whatever powers were left to them to continue the physical abuse. Through all this, Our Lord and his Mother continued to pray for his enemies even though they were causing both of them immeasurable pain and grief. Through it all neither Mother or Son uttered so much as a whisper of complaint. His captors finally tired of their sport, retied him to the pillar and left.

Alone at last in the putrid dungeon he leaned on the pillar as best he could to seek a little rest. During this entire time he was surrounded by a brilliant light. The Angels who had begged earlier to be allowed to free and protect him returned and paid him homage, praising his holy name. They were filled with admiration for what he was doing for his creatures and at the wisdom of his judgments in what he was willing to suffer for them.

The sun was at last beginning to rise and was shining through the small vent near the ceiling. Looking up at the tiny ray of light which was penetrating into the murky darkness of his filthy dungeon, Our Blessed Lord gave thanks to his Eternal Father for the dawn of the day on which mankind would be redeemed.

At this point Our Blessed Lady left the outside of the door to his cell and went up to the fire pit in the vestibule where

---

[86] Our Lord was willing to suffer every cruel torture conceived by the mind of man and demon but Our Blessed Lady would not allow the sexual abuse as that would result in the loss of innocence. In the case of Our Lord this was totally unacceptable and unspeakable and therefore was not allowed at this time or any other. It also speaks to the value of innocence which we as a society value very little. Loss of innocence is never to be taken lightly.

[87] A parent's duty.

a number of people were still gathered. She walked right past them and went into the great hall of the tribunal where her Son had been unjustly condemned. When she reached the spot where he had declared; "I AM! she fainted. John and the women lifted her up and carried her out past the bystanders who said nothing but just watched as if they were in a state of shock.

In his cell, Our Lord prayed to his Eternal Father for his church, the spreading of the faith, for his Apostles; especially Peter who was still in the cave on Mount Olivet weeping over his denials. He prayed for all those who had tortured him, for his Holy Mother and for all in the future who would suffer in his holy name. He offered up all his sufferings and his impending death in atonement for the sins of the world.

Having regained her senses the Blessed Virgin prayed in union with her Divine Son for his church. She also prayed for his enemies with no hint of anger, indignation or dislike toward them; but against the demons she was livid as they were totally devoid of grace and had no redeeming qualities.

Then she addressed a prayer directly to her Divine Son saying; "Divine love of my soul, my Son and Lord, you are worthy to be loved, honored and praised by all creatures since you are the image of the Eternal Father and the figure of his substance; infinite in your being and in your perfections; you are the beginning of all holiness. But if the creatures are to serve you in complete subjection, why do they now, my Lord and God, despise, insult and torture your person which is worthy of the highest worship and admiration? Why has the malice of men risen to such a pitch? Why has pride dared to raise itself even above Heaven? How can envy become so powerful? You are the only unclouded Son of Justice which enlightens and disperses the darkness of sin. You are the fountain of grace withholding its waters from no one. You are the one who in his liberal love gives being and life to all that live upon the earth and all things depend on you, while you have need of none. What then have they seen in your doings? What have they seen in your passion that they should treat you in so vile a manner? O most savage wickedness of sin which has so disfigured your Heavenly beauty and dimmed the light of your Heavenly face. O cruel sin which so inhumanly pursues the repairer of all results of evil.

But I understand, my Son and Master. I understand that you are the builder of true love; the author of human salvation; the Master of all virtues. You wish to put into practice yourself what you teach the humble Disciples of your school. You wish to humble pride, confuse arrogance and become the example of eternal salvation to all and if you desire that all imitate your unspeakable patience and charity, then that is my duty before all others, since I gave you the body which is now subject to suffering, wounds, spit and hard blows. Oh, if only I alone could suffer these pains and that you, my innocent Son be spared. Since this is not possible, let me suffer with you until death. " [88]

Then the Holy Mother addressed herself to the Angels of her guard saying; "Heavenly spirits of my Son, recognize his unchanging deity and the innocence and excellence of his humanity; look to compensate for the injuries and blasphemies heaped upon him by men. Give him glory, magnificence, wisdom, honor, virtue and power. Invite the heavens, the planets, the stars and the elements to acknowledge and confess him and see whether there is another sorrow equal to mine. [89] [90]

The Blessed Virgin exercised great patience during the passion and did not deem her sufferings to be too much in the light of her love for her Divine Son and the depths of his sufferings. She did not deem what she was suffering as a personal injury to herself or as being committed against her. She did not linger on what the outrages were causing her to suffer but only on how they outraged her Divine Son and the negative effect these foul deeds were having on those who committed

---

[88] Quote from the city of God by Mary of Agreda.

[89] Quote from the city of God by Mary of Agreda.

[90] The Blessed Virgin confided to Mary of Agreda that great was the sorrow and most bitter was the grief of my Most Holy Son that not all of mankind should make use of the fruits of his redemption. But next to this sorrow my greatest one was to know that after all these death dealing sufferings of the Lord so many would still damn themselves even within sight of all the infinite treasures of grace. (The Sacraments).

them. She prayed fervently for his persecutors and asked God to free them from their sin and grant them pardon.

While Our Lord was still in his cell, Judas, who had been wandering around in the Hinnom Valley south of the city, entered the fountain gate and made his way up the old Roman steps to the house of the High Priests. He was still holding on to his thirty pieces of silver. As he neared the compound he asked some Temple guards what was going to happen to the Galilean. They told him that he had been condemned to death and would most certainly be crucified. Judas walked slowly around, eavesdropping on peoples conversations concerning all these events. He heard some refer to the cruel treatment his former Master had received and others talk about their amazement at his great patience. He also learned that a second trial was to take place at dawn.

As the sun began to rise, Judas could see that some of the tribunal members were already preparing for the morning trial. Despair was beginning to take possession of his soul and he hid himself in an out of the way place so as not to be seen and recognized. He suddenly became aware that the place where he had taken refuge was occupied by sleeping men. He strained to see in the dim light and was able to make out the form of a cross which these men had prepared for his former Master. At the sight of it he became completely unnerved and was filled with deep feelings of remorse and quickly moved to another spot to await the tribunal.

As soon as it was sufficiently daylight, the council convened again. The chief Priests, Elders and Scribes were looked upon with great respect by the people and they gathered together now for the purpose of giving a semblance of justice to their proceedings as everyone knew fully well that night trials were meaningless under Mosaic Law.

They assembled once again in the great hall in the palace of Ciaphas. Some council members had spent the night as guests of the High Priest while many had gone home and returned at first light. Once everyone was in place the order was given for the guards to bring Our Lord before them once again.

The guards entered the cell and untied Our Lord from the stone pillar while they mocked and jeered at him saying; "Well now, Jesus of Nazareth, see how little your miracles have helped to defend you. The power which you claim to have to rebuild the Temple has failed in securing your escape. Now you will pay for your boldness and your proud ambitions will be brought low. Come now before the Chief Priests and Scribes. They are waiting to put an end to the falsehood you have passed off and deliver you to Pilate who will quickly finish you." [91]

The guards dragged Our Lord before the council who were somewhat taken aback at his shabby appearance. He was covered with mucus and filth which he could not wipe away due to the manner in which his hands were tied. He stood before them horribly disfigured, filling the hall with the putrid smell of manure.

Most of the council wished to condemn Our Lord as quickly as possible but Joseph of Arimathea, Nicodemus and a few others would have none of it. They demanded that any decision in this case should not take place until the Passover festival was over and past, for to proceed now might cause a riot among the people. They also pointed out that no criminal could be unjustly condemned on false charges and to date no crime had been proven as all of the witnesses had contradicted each other.

The High Priests became extremely angry and told Joseph and Nicodemus and their cohorts that they were not surprised to se them taking his side as they deemed them agreeable to Jesus of Nazareth and his doctrines. Ciaphas had all those who seemed favorable towards Our Lord removed from the chamber. [92]

When the courtroom was cleared of all potential friends of the defendant, Ciaphas turned his attention to Our Lord himself. He addressed him sarcastically saying; "If you are the Christ, tells us plainly." Our Lord raised his head and addressed the errant Priest saying; "If I tell you, you will not believe me

---

[91] Quote from the city of God by Mary of Agreda.
[92] The council members removed from the chamber that morning by the actions of Ciaphas never again took their seats on the tribunal in protest of the actions of Ciaphas.

and if I ask you, you will not answer me or let me go; but hereafter the Son of Man will be sitting on the right hand of the power of God." Ciaphas replied;" Then you are the Son of God?" Our Lord said; "You say that I am." [93]

Again they made the determination that they had no more need of witnesses as they had heard it from his own mouth. What was left of the council shouted abusive insults and maltreated him as a low born person with questionable morals who would dare to try and pass himself off as their Messiah and even claim worthiness to sit at God's right hand.

Once again they made certain that he was securely bound and then clasped a chain around his neck. [94] The council members could be heard complaining among themselves that they had to go begging to the Romans to carry out their sentence of death but they knew better than to try to put someone as well known as Our Lord to death on their own without Roman consent. [95] They knew that they were going to have to prove to the Roman Governor that he was an enemy of the Emperor and the Roman Empire. Having condemned him for blasphemy they had to be aware that a religious charge would not bring a sentence of death from the Romans. Last minute details were being ironed out in preparation for bringing Our Lord before the Roman Governor.

The Blessed Virgin and her companions had returned to the Cenacle during the closed trial. John went into her and confessed his guilt in having deserted his beloved Master in the garden and begged her forgiveness which she gave with a heart full of love for this young Apostle.

---

[93] Our Lord is confirming to them that they are correct when they say that he is the Son of God; but they are not concerned with Divine truth, so they deem it blasphemy.

[94] This chain was standard practice for a condemned criminal.

[95] According to Roman law only the Emperor, Senate or Governor of a remote province could use capital punishment. The Romans insisted on a hearing, a defense and a just cause to condemn. In any event this sentence was not even legal under Mosaic Law as judgment was not allowed to be passed on the same day as the trial and certainly not on the eve of the Sabbath. There had been no defense council nor was a defense allowed.

Knowing that the time was at hand when her Divine Son was to be taken to the Romans, she gathered her companions and informed them that it was time to go out into the streets and follow her Son to the end. They set out into the streets of Jerusalem and she asked the Angels of her guard to clear a spot for them so she could see her Son as he was being taken to the Praetorium.

The procession was formed and was now beginning to leave the palace of the High Priest. The council members took the lead, followed by some of the Temple guards, and then Our Lord being dragged, prodded, pulled and pushed by the ever present bailiffs and finally more Temple guards who were followed by a mob.

It was a cold morning and Our Lord was only dressed in his undergarment. The heavy chains were wrapped around his neck and dangled down in front of him slamming into his knees as he walked. He was being hurried along while being beaten, punched and clubbed. He hadn't had any food or water since his capture, except for the sip in the Kidron and the little water the soldier gave him at the gate near Ophel. Having been tormented through the night he hadn't had any sleep and was extremely fatigued.

The curious crowds were increasing by the minute as he was not being forced through the streets by just anyone but by the great Sanhedrin itself, the rulers of the nation. With such dignitaries taking such an interest in this man one could only conclude that they were dealing with the worst of criminals.

The city was overflowing with people not only from all over Israel but from the entire Mediterranean basin who had come to celebrate the Passover. As the crowds began to increase and more people looked upon the procession, each step for Our Lord took on a greater humiliation. Many were completely shocked when they learned who had been arrested and was being taken to the Roman Governor. Some were crying and bewildered while others were screaming for his blood.

As they hurried through the streets, the Holy Mother could hear people talking about her Divine Son. Some of them spoke kindly towards him and were very upset at the events that were taking place. Some were talking about the fate that the leaders of Israel desired for him and about the horrible treatment he was getting. Others referred to all the miracles he had performed and expressed astonishment that he could not escape his tormenters. They were beginning to doubt that his miracles were genuine.

There were people congregating everywhere and the main topic of conversation was the events that were now unfolding concerning Our Lord. The Blessed Virgin was filled with grief but maintained her composure. She again prayed for those who were tormenting her Son and for those whose faith was now being shaken. She implored the Eternal Father and her Divine Son to forgive their sins and to shower them with graces. Even though she had to bear up under the same pains, she harbored no grudges but maintained a loving heart for them willing them nothing but good as they struggled with their faith in him and as his tormentors increased the severity of their blind persecutions.

Some of the people she encountered recognized her and offered their heartfelt sympathy. Others rebuked her for having such a terrible Son. One person boldly admonished her for allowing him to introduce such strange ideas among the people without restraining or dissuading him and told her that at least it would serve as a warning for other mothers, to learn from her misfortune, on how to properly instruct their children. She gratefully accepted the condolences and quietly suffered the rebukes without complaint or answer and continued praying for all of them.

In a short time the Angels conducted her to a spot along the route where they knew he would pass by. She watched intently as the procession slowly approached and then began to pass. When he came into view, even though she was his Mother, she would not have been able to recognize him if it wasn't for his calm demeanor and complete resignation. Loaded down with chains, shackles, spit and manure he was battered beyond even her recognition. Her heart was deeply laden with sorrow as the crowd spewed forth their curses and abusive and filthy language. When he was immediately to her front, she fell prostrate on the ground before him paying him homage; revering and adoring him as no other creature on earth was capable of, alone or collectively. The procession came to a halt. She rose up and Our Lord looked upon her with the depth of his love and a sorrowful affection. She then stepped aside and Our Lord was prodded by his captors to move on. She and her companions joined the procession to follow her Son to the house of the Governor.

As they moved in the direction of the house of the Governor the Holy Mother addressed her Divine Son interiorly, saying; "Most High God and my Son. I am aware of your burning love for men which leads you to hide the infinite power of your Divinity beneath a form of passive flesh, formed in my womb. I confess your incomprehensible wisdom in accepting such affronts and torments and in sacrificing yourself, who are the Lord of all creation, for the rescue of man who is but a servant; dust and ashes. Your goodness is to be praised, blessed, confessed and magnified by all creatures; but how shall I, your Mother ever cease to desire that all these injuries be heaped upon me and not upon your Divine person who are the beauty of the Angels and the glory of the Eternal Father? How shall I cease to desire the end of these pains? With what sorrow is my heart filled to behold you so afflicted; you're most beautiful face so defiled; and when I see that to the Creator and Redeemer alone is denied pity and compassion in such a bitter suffering? But if it is not possible that I relieve you as Mother, do you accept my sorrowful sacrifice in not being able to bring you the relief which is due the true and Holy Son of God." [96] [97]

A small crowd of people from the village of Ophel were gathered in an open space intently watching the procession as it approached. Our Lord had worked many miracles among these poorest of the poor and had instructed them in the way of holiness. But seeing him reduced to such a miserable state shook their faith. Observing this shaken lot the Pharisees began to make fun of them. They were well known to the rulers as most of them

---

[96] Quote from the City of God by Mary of Agreda.

[97] The image of her Divine Son so horribly disfigured was so impressed on the heart and soul of the Blessed Virgin that it remained imprinted in her mind, just as real as she was seeing it now, for the rest of her life.

worked daily in the Temple area." Look at your king now," they jeered: "Do homage to him. Have you no congratulations to offer him now that he is about to be crowned and seated on his throne? All his boasted miracles are at an end. The High Priest has put an end to his tricks and witchcraft. " [98]

They didn't know what to think. They were being told by the rulers of Israel, for whom they had a great deal of respect, that Our Lord was a fraud and deceiver. Some of them walked away but many others couldn't so easily forget all that he had done for them and tried to enter the procession. The Temple guards pushed them aside and prevented them from doing so.

Satan and his demons intently studied all that was taking place. He could feel a power coming out of the infinite patience of this Holy Man that threatened to overcome him. His pride could not accept that such virtue could come from a mere creature and had a nagging suspicion that he was dealing with something more. Still though, he could not bring himself to believe that God would allow himself to be so humiliated or allow himself to be subjected to so much abuse. His fury increased and he increased his efforts to have Our Lord persecuted even more. He simply had to know who this man was for certain. Who was it that was so capable of enduring such horrible suffering without retaliating or even reacting?

The leaders induced the mob to make fun of Our Lord's triumphant entry into Jerusalem at the beginning of the week by mocking his passage through the city now. They mocked him as a king and laid down rags in his path and threw pieces of wood and stones for him to walk on.

They descended Mount Zion, heading north, passed through the village of Acre and turned east toward the Thyropian Valley which ran north and south through the city and passed close to the western Temple wall. They entered the valley near the Temple wall and turned north again in the direction of the Fortress Antonio. At this point, many of the Priests who were in

---

[98] Quote from the Dolorous Passion of Our Lord Jesus Christ by Anne Catherine Emmerich.

the procession left and went off to the Temple to prepare for the Sabbath and the Passover festival. [99]

The Temple Guards struggled to force a path through the ever increasing crowds as the Roman sentries watched intently from the high towers of the Fortress Antonio. A message was quickly sent by the sentries to the Roman Governor that the procession, dragging its prisoner was approaching the Roman compound.

Judas was walking along with the mob and listening to their remarks which held no hope for Our Lord to escape crucifixion. Someone made a remark about the Disciple who had sold him into captivity and how that treachery was more worthy of death than anything the Galilean had done. Some in the mob even had praise for the patience of Our Lord while they in turn trashed Judas and his infidelity. Judas was filled with despair and remorse. [100] He began to think about his betrayal and how it alone had caused all this injustice to be vented upon his former Master. He thought about all the miracles he had seen, the beautiful words he had heard and the benefits he had received from Our Lord. He recalled the sweetness of the Holy Mother and the great love she displayed in trying to attain his conversion. He compared how much he had offended Son and Mother in return for so little gain. All his horrible sins came forward from his soul like an accusing finger. Being without grace since his infamous lips touched Our Lord's Holy face he was left to his own councils. Only the Divine Justice and fairness which is ingrained in our natural reason allowed these thoughts of remorse to come to mind.

---

[99] At about this time of the day the morning sacrifice was taking place in the Temple. It would be the last valid sacrifice of the Old Covenant, ever! Passing by outside the Temple was the Lamb of God, who this day would be the evening sacrifice, establishing the new covenant.

[100] His remorse was not due to repentance for his sin but only for the way things had turned out. He had thought that his actions would gain favor with the ruling powers and that he would gain position, honor and wealth. Instead, he was despised by the rulers and was becoming infamous among the people. The whole treacherous deal had backfired on him.

Satan, who now possessed him, helped things along by suggesting to Judas these truths he was now contemplating, not to bring about his repentance but to convince him that his situation was now hopeless and could not be made right again. He incited Judas to deep sorrow for his misdeeds, pointing out to him his present disgrace among men and filling him with fear of retaliation from his all powerful former Master from whom he could not hide.

Knowing that Judas was vulnerable to suggestion, Satan put the thought into his head to run before anyone in the crowd could recognize him. He should have run ahead to Our Lord, dropped to his knees, confessed his sin and begged his forgiveness; but he did not! He began to run wildly to get away from the crowd at the same time beating his head and cursing himself as the most wretched among men. Satan seeing him in such frenzy put it into his mind to find the Priests, confess his sin and return the silver to them. Judas ran into the Temple and found several of the Priests, who as council members had been at the trial. Thrusting forward his hand which contained the bag with thirty pieces of silver coins, he screamed; "take back your silver; that silver with which you bribed me to betray this just man! Take back your silver; release Jesus! Our compact is at an end! I have sinned grievously for I have betrayed innocent blood."

The Priests answered him with obvious contempt saying: "What have we to do with your sin? If you think you have sold innocent blood it is your affair. We know what we have paid for and we have judged him worthy of death. You have your money, say no more." [101]

Their attitude caused Judas to sink even deeper into despair. He became devoid of all hope and went into a fit of rage. He flung the silver coins onto the Temple floor and turned and ran. He ran south across the city and didn't stop until he was outside the walls and in the Hinnom Valley. Satan remained at

---

[101] The intention of Satan in prodding Judas to do this was to interfere with the condemnation of Our Lord, if possible, as he was still nagged by the uncertainty of whom he was dealing with. His ploy didn't work.

his side constantly tempting him to despair. He reminded Judas how evil this valley was considered and of all the curses the Prophets had placed upon it because Jews of old had sacrificed their own children to the pagan gods here. He heaped torment on torment upon Judas so as to give him the impression that all the curses of the Prophets were directed at him, driving him deeper into despair. Satan whispered into his ear; "Cain, where is your brother Abel? What have you done? His blood cries to me for vengeance. You are cursed upon the earth, a wanderer forever." [102] Judas stumbled eastward and came to the brook Kidron far downstream from the garden of Gethsemane. Gazing across at Mount Olivet the words echoed in his ears; "Friend why have you come? Judas, do you betray your Master with a kiss?

---

[102] Quote from the Dolorous Passion of Our Lord Jesus Christ by Anne Catherine Emmerich.

Chapter IV
The Civil Trials

The procession made its way slowly northward in the direction of the Fortress Antonio. This mighty fortress was a massive square structure which took up two acres of land at its base. The main building itself loomed to a height of sixty feet while the watch towers on all four corners rose above one hundred feet each. It was attached to the northwest corner of the Temple mount and commanded a view of the entire city; especially the Temple and its grounds. The Roman army had quick access to the Temple by way of two stair cases which descended from the southeast tower into the Temple area and also by a connecting underground tunnel. [103] Its use now was to house Roman Soldiers of the *Italica Civium Romanorum Legion, whose* headquarters were in Caesarea, when they were assigned to the Jerusalem fortress to maintain order in the city.

The fortress was located in the southeast corner of a large forum or open space which was used by the Romans as a parade ground and training area. On certain days of the week it was used by the people of Jerusalem as an open air market place. It was surrounded on all sided by colonnades which not only set boundaries for the forum but also supported walkways high in the air which were accessible from the fortress for use by foot patrols. [104]

The Roman Praetorium was just east of the fortress and just to the north of the Great Temple. It contained the Governor's residence when he was in Jerusalem and housed all the official

---

[103] The Romans did not build this fortress. It was originally built by the Maccabees, (See the book of Maccabees in the Old Testament), and was known as the Baris castle. Herod the great had used it for his palace while he was building his new palace on Mount Zion and had remodeled it into the magnificent structure it was at that time. Herod had named it Antonio in honor of his friend and protectorate Roman General Marc Anthony.

[104] This forum was about the size of thirty football fields, covering about thirty acres.

offices of the Roman Government. It was surrounded by terraces on all sides and was connected to the fortress by passage ways and draw bridges. To the north, or front of the Praetorium there was a large courtyard paved with reddish colored stones which was about one third the size of the forum and completely walled in. [105] It is connected to the forum by an archway which after this day is to become known as the "Ecce Homo Arch". This paved courtyard was known as the Lithostrotos (Litho-stro-tos). Within its confines there was a raised platform called Gabbatha from which sentences were proclaimed and in the northwest corner there was a column used for flagellations.

The procession passed by the western side of the fortress and entered the forum. As soon as they passed Antonio, they turned right or east, went through the Ecce Homo Arch and entered the paved courtyard. They then turned south and approached the Praetorium, stopping at a line drawn on the pavement before the northern terrace beyond which the Jewish leaders would not go to avoid defilement. [106]

They seated themselves on benches which the Romans had provided for just such occasions. The bailiffs dragged Our Lord to the foot of the steps leading up to the terrace and stopped.

The Roman Governor, Pontius Pilate, was sitting in a chair on the terrace surrounded by the officers of his tribunal and Roman Soldiers in full military dress. From his judgment seat he looked out with scorn and contempt at the Jewish leaders and the mob they had brought with them. He then turned his attention to their prisoner standing at the bottom of the steps, half naked, battered and bruised from head to foot and loaded down with spit and filth. He stood up and walked to the top of the steps to get a better look.

---

[105] It was about ten acres in size.

[106] The Jewish leaders could not transact business in the house of a pagan without becoming defiled. If they were to become defiled, rituals of penance would have to be performed which would cover a specific number of days before they were made clean again and be able to celebrate the Pasch. There was not enough time before the Passover to do this, so they stopped.

Then he said to the enemies of Our Lord in an angry and contemptible tone; "what have you come about so early? Why have you treated this prisoner so shamefully? Is it not possible to refrain from tearing to pieces and beginning to execute your criminals to this extent even before they are judged? [107]

They did not answer Pilate but ordered the bailiffs to bring Our Lord up the steps to be judged. The brutal bailiffs were only too eager to comply and half prodded and half dragged him up the steps to the terrace. [108]

The Roman Governor had certainly received many reports about this prisoner and his activities as he had gone about his mission preaching and healing throughout his province but had never seen him until now. He was somewhat taken aback by his calmness and the dignity with which he carried himself. Even in spite of his horrid appearance there was something majestic about him which made a quick impression on Pilate. Now, with him standing so near to him he could see clearly just how badly he had been treated at the hands of his captors and it filled him with even more contempt for the Jewish leaders who had disturbed him so early in the day.

Turning his attention to Our Lords captors he informed them that he had no intention of condemning this man without solid proof that their accusations are true. Then he asked them in a voice filled with contempt; "what accusations do you bring against this man? Sensing the Governor's irritation the High Priest replied in a somewhat mournful tone: "If he were not a criminal we would have not delivered him up to you."

They had not expected such a hostile reception from the Governor. They simply wanted him to agree with their decision and get on with the execution so that they could go back to their preparations for the Passover Festival.

---

[107] Quote from the dolorous passion of Our Lord Jesus Christ by Anne Catherine Emmerich.

[108] These marble steps which are known as the "Scala Santa" were eventually brought to Rome and now lead up to one of the entrances to the Basilica of St John Lateran. People usually ascend these steps on their knees.

"Take him and judge him according to your own law," said Pilate. "You know very well," they replied; "that it is not lawful for us to condemn any man to death."

The enemies of Our Lord were becoming more irritated as each moment passed. They had not counted on this turn of events. The Governor was balking at condemning Our Lord when they had hoped that he would just rubber stamp their decision.

After some deliberate thought, Pilate ordered them to produce their accusations. They first accused Our Lord of perverting the nation and disturbing its peace and tranquility. Then they had witnesses testify that he had violated and desecrated the Sabbath by curing the sick on that most holy day. Pilate sneered that it was very evident that none of them had been sick or they would not have complained about being healed on the Sabbath. Ignoring this they brought forth more witnesses that he seduced the people and introduced vile doctrines such as no one could attain eternal life unless they eat his flesh and drink his blood. Pilate retorted by telling them that apparently they wished to follow his doctrines as they are thirsting for both his body and his blood.

The enemies of Our Lord finally caught on that if they were going to get anywhere with Pilate, they were going to have to make him believe that Our Lord conspired against Rome and the Emperor so they dropped the religious accusations and moved on to political ones. But in their haste they almost made a fatal blunder. They accused Our Lord of forbidding people to pay tribute (taxes) to the Emperor to which Pilate quickly replied that they were lying and that apparently he knew more about these events than they did. [109]

They quickly changed the subject and accused him of declaring himself a king. Then they had witnesses testify that even though Our Lord was of lowly birth, he has become the head of a great multitude and that he has threatened to destroy Jerusalem. They further testified that his followers had attempted

---

[109] Ultimate responsibility for collecting taxes fell to Pilate as the Provincial Governor. Without thinking they had just accused him of not doing his job.

once to make him a king but he had fled from them as it was not yet time for this according to his plans. [110] They claimed that lately he was coming out more into the public eye and had made a great spectacle of himself by coming into Jerusalem riding a white colt amid much fanfare in which great crowds hailed him as the Son of David. They claimed that he requires his followers to give him kingly homage and that he claims to be the anointed one; the Messiah; the king of the Jews which has been long promised. [111]

This final charge caused Pilate to become thoughtful and aroused some concern. He was a very superstitious man and was well versed on the gods of Rome and the religion of the Jews. He knew very well that the Prophets had long promised a deliverer; one who would free them from slavery; a Messiah! He was also well aware that the Jewish people firmly believed in all these prophecies.

Pilate turned to Our Lord and said; "What do you answer to these accusations they bring against you?" But he wouldn't answer Pilate in front of his enemies. The Governor was astonished at his silence and the patient calmness by which he seemed to be unaffected by their tirades and outbursts. Once again he was momentarily lost in his own thoughts. Then without anymore testimony Pilate abruptly left the terrace and went into the Praetorium.

The Blessed Mother had begged the Eternal Father to keep her within sight of her Divine Son as far as was naturally possible until the end of his passion and her request had been readily granted. As a result the Holy angels of her guard cleared the way for her and her companions so that they were in a spot where they could hear the whole interview with Pilate. She shielded her face with her mantle so that no one could see the immense suffering she was enduring by the sorrow which

---

[110] They were speaking of the incident when he had fed the five thousand and they wanted to declare him king but he went through their midst and left. (Luke, Chap: 9 Vs: 10-17).

[111] These things to which they referred were all lies as Our Lord never claimed or demanded any of these which they accused him of.

pierced her Immaculate Heart. At times she shed tears of blood as she suffered the same interior and physical sufferings meted out to her loving Son. At the same time she practiced all the virtues Our Lord was expressing in unison with her suffering Son and God. Hearing all the unjust, lying accusations leveled at her Son she regarded it as an act of justice that his innocence be made known to all. She prayed earnestly that Pilate would be given the grace necessary to see his innocence and due to these prayers, Pilate saw clearly that Our Lord was a victim of envy and hatred. [112] Also because of her prayers, Our Lord would be more open with Pilate.

Pilate sent an order that Our Lord alone was to be brought to him inside the Praetorium. He thought about the story of how the kings of the east had made inquiries of King Herod years ago as to the location of the new king born to the Jews and that Herod had ordered a slaughter of babies in order to kill him.

Pilate studied Our Lord intently as he was brought into his presence. He knew with certainty that he was not now a reigning king, for Rome controlled all such matters within its Empire. Never the less he needed to know if this man claimed such a right or actually had a right to kingship. His majestic appearance even in his present humbled state caused Pilate to wonder.

"Are you the King of the Jews?" Pilate questioned. Without his enemies present, Our Lord answered immediately; "do you say this thing of yourself or have others told you of me?" "Am I a Jew?" said Pilate; "your own Nation and the Chief Priests have delivered you up to me as deserving of death. What have you done?" Our Lord answered; "my kingdom is not of this world. If my kingdom were of this world my servants would certainly fight that I not be handed over to the Jews; but now my kingdom is not from here." Pilate said in a more serious tone; "so you are a king then!" Our Lord replied; "You say that I am a

---

[112] Although he proclaimed Our Lord's innocence many times during the trials, in the end Pilate did not properly respond to this truth made known to him or the grace granted to him.

king.[113] For this was I born and for this I came into the world, to bear witness to the truth. Everyone who is of the truth hears my voice." "Pilate said to him what is truth?" [114]

They went back out onto the terrace where his enemies were waiting impatiently. Pilate had not fully understood what Our Lord had told him but he knew that he was no danger to the Emperor or to his own province. Addressing the Chief Priests he said; "I find no cause in him." His accusers were enraged and began making one accusation after another shouting out at the same time. Our Lord said nothing through all this but continued praying for his tormentors.

Pilate was still running over in his head the answers Our Lord had given him while they were inside and was completely amazed at how badly his enemies wanted him dead. He knew they wouldn't be pleased with any other outcome but he was convinced that they had delivered him up only out of hatred and envy. He thought their accusations were not only false but ridiculous to boot.

Pilate said to Our Lord; "Do you answer nothing? Look at how many things they accuse you of. I see plainly that all they allege is false." Over hearing what Pilate said to Our Lord the Priests became livid with anger and screamed; "you find no cause in him? Is it no crime to incite the people to revolt in all parts of the kingdom; to spread his false doctrines not only here but in Galilee also?"

Hearing the reference to Galilee, Pilate asked if Our Lord was a Galilean. They told him that he was born in Galilee and grew up there. [115] Also that he had lived with his parents in Nazareth and now lived in Capharnaum.

Pilate thought for a moment. In their haste to condemn him they had provide him with a chance to be rid of the whole

---

[113] Our Lord is saying to Pilate that he is correct in saying that he is a king.

[114] What a sadly ironic question. The truth is standing right in front of him.

[115] This plainly shows the results of an improper religious trial as they think he was born in Galilee. Proper investigation and a proper defense would have established the fact that he had been born in Bethlehem from which the Messiah was expected. There could have been a much different result if the Sanhedrin had properly established his origin.

affair. He knew that Herod Antipas was anxious to see Our Lord and thought that maybe he would see through their phony accusations and set Our Lord free. That would eliminate the need of passing sentence himself. Herod just happened to be in Jerusalem for the celebration of the Passover and Our Lord was one of his subjects. Herod, he concluded, could judge him right away and have it done with.

Pilate said to the Priests; "take him to Herod." Then he sent one of his officer's ahead to inform Herod that Jesus of Nazareth was being sent to him for judgment.

While this first hearing before Pilate had been taking place his wife Claudia Procula had sent him messages that she needed to talk to him. Now she came out onto the terrace and watched the cruel treatment vented upon Our Lord by his captors who were angry at having been rebuked by Pilate in front of this large crowd of people. Further more they were humiliated at having to go begging to Herod with whom they had a poor relationship because of his marital situation. They tied Our Lord up again using even more cruel measures than before and renewed their curses and abuses even more intently displaying their anger at this new delay as if it was their captors fault, Claudia Procula watched their actions and was horrified.

The new palace of Herod Antipas was directly north of the Praetorium and it took about an eight to ten minute walk to reach it. The procession formed up once again and went north through the sheep gate [116] toward Mount Bethesda and the palace of Herod. Pilate sent a small group of Roman soldiers with them to witness the trial before Herod as he did not trust the Jewish leaders. [117]

The Temple guards clear the path through the crowd while Our Lord is attended by the ever present bailiffs. The scribes, Pharisees and Priests walk close by as they force Our Lord to move along at a very fast pace causing him more pain and discomfort.

---

[116] Formerly known as the gate of Benjamin.

[117] This is the first time that Roman soldiers take an active part in the passion. Even now they are only along as observers.

The Angels of her guard continued to clear a path so that the Blessed Virgin and her companions could stay close enough to Our Lord to keep him in sight. She wished to stay constantly in his presence even though it brought her fuller participation in all his sorrows and torments. All the filthy curses, insults and reproaches fell on her virginal ears while she witnessed all that happened to her Divine Son and absorbed in her own body all the pains, torments and beatings he was suffering.

In the palace of Herod, the messenger Pilate had sent informed him that Our Lord was on his way to be judged by him and this pleased Him very much. He had received many reports concerning Our Lord's preaching and miracles and was aware that he was closely connected to John the Baptist whom he had killed. He especially wanted to see Our Lord work a miracle with all the expectation of a small child awaiting a magic show.

When the procession arrived Herod was seated on a throne surrounded by his councilors and his own private soldiers. [118] The enemies of Our Lord entered and placed themselves close to Herod's throne leaving Our Lord in the entrance.

The Blessed Virgin and her party were not allowed to enter into Herod's palace. She informed John that she wished to go back and visit the major points of the passion to date. John led the group back to the places which had been sanctified by the presence of Our Lord. They visited the houses of Annas and Ciaphas, the village of Ophel, Gethsemane and the Garden of Olives. They stopped, prayed and wept at places where he had fallen or suffered dreadful torments. On many occasions the Holy Mother knelt down and kissed the ground made holy by her suffering Son. Mary Magdalene was filled with grief and John

---

[118] They were mostly German Mercenaries. As King of Galilee Herod was allowed to maintain a private army for his own protection. There were three armies in Palestine during this time period in history. Herod's army, the Temple guard and the Roman army. Herod's Army and the Temple Guard were of sufficient size to maintain order but were never allowed to be large enough to pose a threat to the Roman Army.

tried as best he could to console his companions while trying to fight back his own tears. [119]

While the majority of the inhabitants of the city were gathering around the palace of Herod, Pilate went together with his wife to a small garden building on the terrace behind the Praetorium which faced the Temple compound. Claudia Procula was highly agitated and filled with much fear. She pleaded with Pilate not to let any harm come to Our Lord. She then related to Pilate all that she had suffered in visions which she had endured during the night

She had been shown the major events in Our Lord's life, the annunciation, the nativity, the adoration of the shepherds and kings, the prophecies of Simeon and Anna, the flight into Egypt and the massacre which followed plus the temptation in the wilderness. She had also seen the major events of his public life.

In her dreams he was always surrounded by a splendid light while his enemies appeared in hideous forms. She had been shown his intense sufferings and the exceptional patience and love with which he endured these torments. She was also allowed to witness the anguish of his Mother and her total acceptance of his fate. She related to her husband how these visions had filled her with a terrible feeling of dread.

Then when the night was over and dawn came she was awakened by the noise of the crowd and when she rose from her bed and looked out the window and saw the procession dragging a battered and bloody man toward the terrace she was stunned to see the man in her dreams. She was overwhelmed by the sight and had immediately sent him the messages.

What Claudia did not know was that Satan and his demons were responsible for her terrible visions. They still could not determine at this point whether or not they were just dealing with an exceptional holy man or a God-Man. They are still confused by the manner in which he endures this great suffering

---

[119] Even before the passion was complete the Blessed Virgin and her companions set the stage for the pious devotion which would later be known as the "stations of the cross". Through the remainder of her life the Holy Mother would practice this devotion.

with such patience. In their pride, they cannot bring themselves to believe that God could so humble himself as to endure these insults without using his power to prevent it.

They are, however, convinced that some great mystery was unfolding in the midst of mankind which would cause great problems with their evil designs if it was not stopped. Satan had tried many times to influence Our Lord's enemies to end their persecutions but to no avail. So now they turn to tormenting Claudia so that she can influence Pilate who is struggling with many doubts.

Pilate was upset by what his wife was revealing to him. He compared her story with all the things that he had previously heard about Our Lord. He reflected on the deep hatred exhibited against this man and his silence amid this swarm of accusations made against him. He recalled the answers he had received to his questions and how he had not fully understood them. He finally told his wife that he had already made up his mind that Our Lord was innocent; that the accusations leveled against him were all lies and that he would not condemn him. [120]

Herod was very pleased that Pilate had sent Our Lord to him to be judged because Pilate was publicly acknowledging his right of jurisdiction over Galileans. Not only that, but he had wanted for a long time to see this man of whom John the Baptist had spoken so highly and of whom the Herodians [121] had submitted so many reports. He had often sent many agents into the field to observe and report on Our Lord's activities and was now overjoyed at the opportunity to interrogate him in front of the whole court and the leaders of the Nation.

However, when he looked at Our Lord standing in the entrance to his court he was filled with mixed emotions. He was glad to see him humiliated as he had never seen fit to appear before his court but at the same time he was disgusted at the sight

---

[120] Pilate was a morally corrupt man and a very indecisive individual. He was superstitious and used charms and spells while consulting the false gods of Rome when he had to make a difficult decision. His main concern was himself and how things would turn out for him. This came before fairness or justice.

[121] The political party which supported the Herod family.

of him battered, bloody and covered with spittle and manure. He ordered the Priests to take him out of his presence and to return him cleaned of all his disgusting filth.

The Temple guards and the bailiffs promptly took Our Lord to an outer courtyard and placing cold water in a vessel, quickly scrubbed what little clothes he still had on and then roughly scrubbed his face and body with absolutely no regard for his many open wounds or to the pain and discomfort their actions caused. [122]

While Our Lord was being cleaned up Herod used the occasion to insult and chastise the Priests. He was terribly upset with the Priests for having excommunicated him for marrying his brother's wife. Due to their actions he was not able to fully participate in the Temple rituals and Jewish holidays. This humiliation of the Priests, added to their already pent up anger at all these delays, which they regarded as an insult to their very capable judgment to begin with.

When Our Lord was returned to the court, Herod offered him some refreshment but he refused it and turned his head away. So Herod began to question Our Lord saying; "Is it possible, Jesus of Nazareth, that it is you yourself that appears before me as a criminal? I have heard your actions so much spoken of. The Roman Governor has sent you to me to be judged. What answer can you give to all these accusations? Your are silent? I have heard much concerning your wisdom and the religion you teach; let me hear you answer and confound your enemies. Are you King of the Jews? Are you the Son of God? Who are you? You are said to have performed wonderful miracles; work one now in my presence. I have the power to release you. Is it true that you restored sight to the blind; raised up Lazarus from the dead and fed two or three thousand people with a few loaves? Why do you not answer? I recommend you to work a miracle quickly before me! Perhaps you may rejoice afterwards at having complied with my wishes. Who are you? Where has your power come from? How is it that you no longer

---

[122] In all probability they scrubbed his clothes while still on his body leaving them soaking wet on this very chilly morning.

posses it? Are you he, whose birth was foretold in such a wonderful manner? Kings from the east came to my father to see a newly born king of the Jews. Is it true that you were that child? Did you escape when so many children were massacred and how was your escape managed? Why have you been for so many years, unknown? Answer my questions! Are you a king? Your appearance is certainly not regal. I have been told that you were conducted to the Temple in triumph a short time ago. What was the meaning of such an exhibition? Speak out at once! Answer me! [123]

Unlike Pilate who was astonished at the calmness and silence of Our Lord, Herod was becoming upset by it. Seeing his anger building the Priests and Elders began once again to make their rapid fire accusations with which they had bored Pilate to death. Herod all but ignored them. He knew that their ends were purely political and even though he was very angry at Our Lord's refusal to answer [124] he was not going to give them the decision they wanted.

Herod had misunderstood the motives of Pilate in that he had sent Our Lord to him hoping that he would agree with his finding of innocent and set him free without any further need of hearings. Herod had made up his mind from the beginning that he would agree with Pilates finding and send him back to the governor as a good will gesture. Another factor that swayed his decision was that he felt an unexplained fear in the presence of Our Lord and still had guilty feelings over the death of John the Baptist. Last but not least he thoroughly despised the Priests and was not going to find in their favor for any reason.

Herod, therefore, found Our Lord to be without guilt in all that he was accused of but because of his refusal to answer his questions found him guilty of being a fool and instructed his

---

[123] Quote from the Dolorous Passion of Our Lord Jesus Christ by Anne Catherine Emmerich.
[124] Our Lord would not speak to Herod or even look at him because of his adulterous union with Herodias and because he had beheaded John the Baptist. He had made himself unworthy to hear the author of life.

soldiers and servants, about two hundred in number, to take this fool away and to give him the honors due to a fool.

They took possession of Our Lord and dragged him back out into the courtyard in which he had been scrubbed and which spanned the distance between the two major portions of the palace. Herod watched as his paid stooges' heaped insult after insult upon Our Lord by reviling, mocking, punching and kicking him. They took hold of his lead ropes and dragged him rapidly around the courtyard bouncing him off the walls and columns.

While Our Lord was being tormented by Herod's soldiers and servants, Annas and Ciaphas tried to persuade Herod to pass a death sentence. Herod replied loud enough to insure that the Roman soldiers could hear him, telling the Priest it would be wrong if I condemn him, inferring that he agreed with Pilate's decision of innocence.

The Priests were finally convinced that they had reached a dead end with Herod and that any further argument was pointless. They sent some of their servants into the section of the city called Acre where most of the Pharisees lived with instructions that the Pharisees should gather up the rabble of the city and congregate with them in the area of the Praetorium and to bribe them to create an uproar and to demand the death of the Nazarene. They also sent messengers into other parts of the city to stir up the people with threats of Divine vengeance if they did not demand the death of this blasphemer. Their servants were also instructed to tell lies, such as that Herod had found him guilty and that if he were not executed he would join the Romans and use his power to help destroy the Nation.

They also had money distributed among Herod's soldiers in an attempt to get them to treat him badly enough to bring about his death as they were very afraid that Pilate would let him go instead of condemning him to death.

Herod's soldiers obtained a large white feed sack and cut holes in it for the head and arms to fit through and dressed Our Lord in it. It was a custom to clothe mentally ill people in white so that other people would recognize their deficiency and treat them as a fool. Then they continued to ruthlessly drag him from pillar to post, slamming him against the walls and columns in an attempt to bring about his death as they had been paid to do.

Then they threw a scarlet robe over his shoulders and mocked him as a king repeatedly hitting him on the head with sticks. Just about all the soldiers and servants of Herod took part in amusing themselves by heaping torment after torment upon him. Our Lord occasionally emitted a feeble moan or groan while looking upon his tormentors with loving compassion as he continued to pray for them. Now and then he was felled by blows and would have died if Angels had not intervened and anointed his head with Heavenly ointments.

When the Priests were satisfied that all the orders they had given out were being complied with they tried one last time to get Herod to condemn Our Lord to death. He steadfastly refused their request and immediately issued orders that he be returned to Pilate dressed in his fools robe.

Herod then sent the messenger back to Pilate to thank him for the courtesy shown to him in sending Our Lord to him to be judged and that he agreed with the Governor's judgment finding no guilt in him.

The captors of Our Lord were more annoyed than ever at having to return him to Pilate because Herod refused to condemn him to death especially since they knew that Pilate was not willing to condemn him himself.

The Blessed Mother and her companions had returned by the time they brought Our Lord out of the palace. Although she had not been allowed to be present she had still witnessed and suffered all that her Son had suffered. As he was taken past her, a look of deep love and sorrow passed between Mother and Son. The white garment in which they had dressed him pierced her soul with new sorrow as she understood that they were displaying the God of all creation as a mentally ill fool; but what she knew that they did not, was that in their ignorant folly they had clothed him in the color of holiness and innocence. She adored her Divine Son with a deep reverence; a reverence of which no other creature in the entire world was capable of.

Our Lord continued praying for his tormentors and in his deep humility he kept repeating the words of David which were written centuries before; "I am a worm and no man, the reproach of men and the outcast of people. All they that saw me have laughed me to scorn; they have spoken with their lips and wagged their heads."

His enemies decided to take him back by a longer route then the one that they had come by to allow more time for the messengers they had dispatched to different parts of the city to do their dirty work. They also wanted to parade him through different parts of the city so that people could see him reduced to his present miserable state. [125]

The white fool's robe that Herod's soldiers had put on him was too long and at times he would get his feet tangled up in the hem and go crashing to the ground. Instead of helping him up his captors hit and kicked him each time until he rose on his own. On several occasions they tripped him on purpose or violently threw him to the ground by yanking on his guide ropes. The crowd was pressing in so tightly that at times people would walk on his body and even his face when he fell. Many used the falls as an occasion to deliver many kicks as he lay on the ground or struggled to get up. His enemies were greatly pleased by these actions of the crowd. The brutal bailiffs and Temple Guards found it to be an occasion of entertainment and laughed and carried on as if they were at a party and Our Lord was a piñata.

He endured all this malice in complete silence. He implored his Eternal Father to provide him the grace and energy he needed to persevere to the end to bring about our redemption.

The Blessed Virgin was moved to the deepest compassion and sorrow as she witnessed these indignities and atrocities. She instructed the Angels of her guard to collect the Sacred Blood of

---

[125] They could not have gone north as it would have taken them away from the Praetorium and the city. They did not go south as this would have been the path they had come by. It is doubtful that they went east as that would have led into the Kidron Valley where there would have been no one to parade him in front of. It is most likely that they went west on the Joppa road and then turned south on a very rough road which wasn't used much and came back into the city either through the gate of Ephraim (fish gate) or the Garden Gate on the western wall near Calvary. Either gate would have brought them through a portion of the city and taken more time.

her Divine Son so that people couldn't walk on it. They promptly complied. Then she instructed them to bring her petition to her Son that these Holy Angels of her guard be allowed to carry out her command of preventing people from walking on his Sacred Body as this act of irreverence caused her deep anguish as his Mother. The Angels presented this petition to Our Lord in her holy name and he granted this request and instructed the Angels to fulfill her desire. For the rest of the journey to the Praetorium the Angels would not allow Our Lord to be tripped, thrown down or walked on. However, they did not interfere with the usual torments of hitting, clubbing, slapping, kicking, spitting and smearing with mud and manure. [126]

They finally reached the paved courtyard of the Praetorium. The crowd had swelled considerably throughout the morning and the Pharisees and servants of the Priests could be seen walking back and forth trying to incite the people to do their bidding.

Pilate watched from the terrace as the procession slowly made its way through the crowd. While they had been before the tribunal of Herod, Pilate had been talking to some of the servants and confidants of the Priests and High Priests regarding freeing a prisoner in keeping with the Passover feast. He wanted them to persuade the Priests to ask for the Nazarene and to be content with a punishment that he was willing to inflict. Pilate was a little upset with Herod for not disposing of the matter and sending Our Lord back to him for judgment but now he knew that he must deal with this situation himself.

Pilate carefully observed the crowd before him. It was swelling by the minute and was showing signs of becoming unruly. Fearing that an insurrection was becoming a possibility he sent a message to the Fortress Antonio for the troops to go on full alert and to deploy in the forum in full combat gear. They were not to make any hostile moves but were to form up and

---

[126] It is difficult enough to endure the indignity of being smeared with mud and manure but one can only imagine the discomfort caused by the acid content of mud and manure spread on open wounds.

await his orders. At this time he only wished to make a show of force. [127]

The procession finally made its way to the bottom of the terrace steps and the Priests took their seats on the benches provided for them.

As the four bailiffs attempted to drag Our Lord up the white marble steps his feet became entangled in his makeshift garment and he fell hard, cracking his head and drawing blood. Laughter went up from the crowd and the bailiffs beat him instead of helping him. They finally dragged him up to the terrace where he could be seen by all.

Pilate, who had been seated in his chair, rose and came forward to the edge of the terrace and said: you have brought this man before me accusing him of perverting the people by his doctrines and having examined him in your presence I was not convinced of the truth of your accusations. Herod, to whom I have sent him and before whom you repeated your accusations refused to condemn him to death. I will chastise him, therefore and release him. [128]

The Priests flew off their benches in a fit of anger. The Pharisees moved about among the people trying to incite a revolt. The crowd became highly excited but was not yet ready to revolt with a thousand heavily armed soldiers standing by who were deployed between them and the only escape route.

A portion of the crowd pushed forward and Pilate raised his hands above his head giving the signal for silence. When the crowd had quieted down one of them yelled out for Pilate to

---

[127] The Jewish historian Flavius Josephus sets the number of Roman soldiers in Jerusalem at this particular time at one thousand. In all probability this is the first cohort of the legion. The average cohort was staffed with six centuries or six hundred men. The first cohort of each legion was staffed with a thousand men or ten centuries. These were generally the best troops in the legion.

[128] Pilate, knowing that Our Lord was innocent and that his enemies were deeply hostile towards him was not willing to sentence him to death at this time. He reasoned that a severe scourging, known as the half death, might satisfy them.

grant them the favor he always granted them on the festival day. [129]

In response to this request Pilate addressed the crowd again and said; "It is customary for me to deliver to you a criminal at Passover time. Who will you that I release to you? Barabbas or Jesus who is called the Christ. [130]

The crowd became silent except for a few feeble half hearted calls for Barabbas. Pilate knew immediately that he had struck a nerve.

As the crowed pondered its choices a servant came up to Pilate with a message from his wife. He left the terrace for a moment to confer with the servant. Claudia Procula had sent him to remind Pilate of his earlier pledge not to condemn this man. He sent the servant back to his wife to tell her that he would keep his pledge.

The Holy Mother stood in a corner of the courtyard with her close companions, weeping. Even though she knew that the redemption of mankind could not be brought about in any other way, she was filled with immeasurable grief and a motherly desire for him to escape torture and death. She prayed to the Eternal Father not to allow it to happen. She prayed in the same way her Divine Son prayed in the garden, if it is possible let this chalice pass away. She faintly hoped that it was true that Pilate wished to release him but as always she accepted the will of the Father in union with her Son and Lord.

There was a group of people close by who were from the city of Capharnaum where Our Lord had not only lived and

---

[129] For a long time it had been the custom of the Jews, as an act of thanksgiving to God for freeing them from Egypt, to free the worst offender in custody and to forgive all his crimes. When they wrote their treaties with the Romans, the Romans agreed to honor it and did. It is most likely that the person making this request was favorable to Our Lord and was hoping that he would be released.

[130] Pilate is being shrewd here. He offers no other choices, only these two. St Luke and St Mark say in sedition he committed murder. St Matthew calls him a notorious murderer. St John calls him a murderer. Barabbas terrorized the city for months before he was finally caught. Pilate knows that he is the worst criminal in the dungeon and that the people do not want him back on the streets.

taught but performed many miracles. They cast a quick glance at the Blessed Virgin now and then but for the most part they pretended that they didn't know her.

Pilate returned to his chair on the terrace and seated himself. Once again he demanded; "which of these two am I to deliver to you? This time the crowd screamed for Barabbas, including the group from Capharnaum. "But what am I to do with Jesus who is called the Christ?" Pilate asked. The crowd responded; "let him be crucified! Let him be crucified! Pilate answered; "Why? What evil has he done? I find no cause in him. I will scourge him and then release him." But the crowd screamed all the more; "Crucify him! Crucify him! The Priests and Pharisees encouraged them running back and forth among the people as if having a fit. [131]

Pilate looked out over the crowd for a long moment, amazed at their hateful frenzy. He finally gave in to their wishes and had Barabbas released but he still refused to condemn Our Lord and ordered him to be scourged. [132]

This scourging ordered by the Governor is an official act of the Roman State and it is to be conducted under Roman authority. Therefore Roman soldiers now take custody of Our Lord and clear a path through the crowd to the northwest corner of the paved courtyard and up to a column used for scourging. However they allowed the bailiffs to maintain physical custody as they pushed and pulled Our Lord through the courtyard in the midst of the Roman escort.

When they arrive at the pillar, the bailiffs released the ropes and stepped back out of the way while the soldiers formed a perimeter around the area of the column to keep the public out. Only some of the Jewish leaders were allowed close enough to witness the scourging.

---

[131] Once again the Jewish leaders were in violation of the law by asking for Barabbas. The law required the release of the worst criminal and since they regarded Our Lord as the worst one, they should have asked for him.

[132] Pilate did not order this scourging as a preparation for crucifixion but as a punishment in place of crucifixion to try to satisfy his enemies without employing a death sentence.

From a guard house behind the Fortress Antonio which was located in the eastern end of the forum, six lictors [133] come forward carrying their whips and rods and drop their scourges at the base of the column. First they untied Our Lord and then roughly tore off the mock scarlet cloak put on him by Herod's soldiers. Then they ordered him to finish undressing himself. He quickly obeyed and removed all his undergarments except for a scanty cloth that covered his private parts. When the lictors and the bailiffs tried to remove it from him their arms would not function. They finally gave up trying and again blamed it on sorcery as the bailiffs had done in his cell beneath the house of Ciaphas.

Under Jewish Law, no criminal could receive more than forty lashes but was generally given thirty nine to be sure that the law was complied with. Under Roman law their was no set limit and very often, a criminal was scourged to death. Our Lord would be scourged under Roman law and the number of stripes to be inflicted is an open issue.

The lictors punched him a few times and then threw him up against the pillar. Our Lord stood before the pillar with every muscle in his body quivering not only from the cold morning air but also from the non stop brutal treatment he had been subjected to without end.

There was an iron ring near the top of the pillar and he raised his battered and bloody hands up to it to offer himself in sacrifice. They securely tied his hands to the iron ring pulling him up onto the tips of his toes. They then tied his feet to the column so he wouldn't twist around. [134]

---

[133] These six men belong to a group of about fifty condemned men who perform the duties of executioner when called upon. The soldiers stand guard and maintain order while these men do the whipping and crucifying. These six specialize in scourging.
[134] Our Lord now stands bound and naked before all present. He is about to pay the penalty for the sins of lust and impurity, adultery, fornication, masturbation, same gender sex, pornography, prostitution, artificial birth control, abortion, lustful thoughts, lustful entertainment, etc. He had foreseen this penalty the night before in the Garden and it had caused him to sweat

With Our Lord securely bound to the column two of the lictors take up their position near him, one to the right and one to the left. They have done this many times before and they know how to whip their prisoner in rhythmic fashion so as not to interfere with one another. In their hands, they each have a Roman flagellum. [135]

The signal to begin is given by a Roman officer and the whips come crashing against his body in their ghoulish rhythmic fashion. The pain inflicted by the led balls is excruciating to the point of paralysis. Each time the lead balls land they rupture the tiny blood vessels beneath the skin causing globules of blood to form into large welts.

They beat him on the shoulders, rib cage and buttocks mercilessly. The lead balls crash against his hips and legs with all the strength they can put into each blow. Again, again and again the lead balls come whistling through the air and smash against his already battered and abused flesh. The pain is worse than fire as his muscles begin to cramp and spasm. For what must seem like an eternity the landing of the lead balls over and over and over again up and down the entire expanse of his body are inflicted without pity or the slightest hint of compassion.

Finally the lictors stop on their own, their muscles weary as they gasp for breath. Our Lord is covered from head to foot with welt upon welt with some of them already oozing blood.

Two more lictors step up to take the place of the first ones. These two are armed with rods about two feet long and they begin beating him in the same rhythmic manner without giving him any chance at recovery. The blows from the rods rupture the welts and blood globules, splattering blood every where with every stripe. It spattered on the column, the stone pavement and all over the lictors. The blows fell in perfect

---

blood. Naked are these sins committed without shame or remorse and naked shall the penalty be paid in shame and humiliation.

[135] A wooden handled whip with three leather thongs attached which were embedded with lead balls in the shape of a tiny dumbbell. Each stripe will land three dumbbells against the body which are designed to rupture the tiny blood vessels beneath the skin and cause blood globules to form under the skin.

unison, rupturing, spattering and wounding. Again and again the rods fell against his body as the lictors plied their trade as if they were in a demonic fury with no thought to mercy. They beat and beat and beat from head to foot in every place they first two had placed welts to be sure that they opened every welt and globule.

During this time, Pilate was still trying to deal with those who wanted Our Lord dead. While he was trying to negotiate with some of the Jewish leaders the High Priest came to the lictors and gave them money and intoxicating drink to bribe them to increase their cruelty and to bring about his death at the column as they still had fears that Pilate might release him.

The crowds were kept some distance from the flagellation by the Roman soldiers. Some just wandered back and forth while others watched the haggling between Pilate and their leaders. Now and then Pilate signaled for silence from the crowd. During these lulls the sound of whips could be heard slamming against Our Lord's mangled body mingled with the moans and groans he occasionally emitted. At times, the bleating of the lambs which were being washed in the Probatica pool, which was not far off, for the Paschal sacrifice could be heard in unison with the sounds of the flagellation.

His Blessed Mother stood in a corner of the paved courtyard with her companions and although she was not allowed near the column, witnessed all that was happening to him in visions which God granted her and felt every sting of every blow in her virginal body. While she did not show the wounds as her Son did, she became so disfigured by what she was going through that she hardly looked like her natural self, even to her companions. No words could express the suffering in her soul in knowing the innocence and purity of her most Holy Son and the unimaginable pain and anguish he was enduring for the love of the ungrateful beings who had committed these sins of lust. All the vile curses and comments which fell upon her ears pierced her soul to the very depths of it existence. She groaned feebly and wept tears of blood. Her strength was failing her and she was being heavily supported by her older sister, Mary of Heli. [136]

The blood was now flowing freely down Our Lord's body onto the stone pavement. His blood spattered everywhere as the continual blows found their mark and spotted the lictors from head to foot. They beat him until they were so exhausted they could beat him no more and then gave way to the third pair.

These two lictors had a different flagellum than the first two. Instead of lead balls the thongs on their whip were embedded with small metal hooks for ripping and tearing the flesh. They set to work in the same rhythmic manner as the lictors before them cutting ripping and tearing his bleeding body ripping off pieces of flesh which fell to the ground. In a short time his entire body was one large open bleeding an mangled wound. Flesh was torn from his shoulders and rib cage to the point that his bones were plainly visible. By the time these two lictors stopped he was one large mass of wounds and flesh hung in chards from his shoulders, rib cage, buttocks and legs. If he had not been securely tied to the ring above his head he would have fallen limply to the ground.

The lictors untied his feet from the pillar but not because they intended to let him go. They simply turned him around and placed his back against the column and retied his feet. Then they tied a rope around his waist to keep him from sagging forward as they fully intended to repeat the process on his front side.

The first two lictors who had scourged his back side retook their places with the lead balled flagellum and began whipping him once again. They savagely beat him on the chest, waistline, hips, loins, legs and ankles. Stripe after stripe, lash upon lash and blow upon blow the whips fell until there was no place left to land a blow that wasn't filled with welts. His body

---

[136] Mary of Heli was about twenty years older than the Blessed Virgin and was also the daughter of Anna and Joachim or in Hebrew, Heliachim. She was called Mary of Heli because she was the daughter of Heliachim. She was married to Cleophus and had a daughter who was called Mary of Cleophus who was the niece of the Blessed Virgin. She was married to a man called Alpheus. They had three sons, Simon, James and Jude who all became apostles.

was a mass of welts, bruises and black and blue marks by the time they stopped.

The lictors with the rods came forward and pounded him with blow after savage blow and as before the Sacred Blood spattered everywhere and spotted everything close by. They beat his chest, hips, loins, legs, and ankles in an attempt to rupture every welt and globule where every lead ball had left its mark. They repeatedly beat his face until his features were distorted beyond any hope of recognition. They made it a point to beat his hands and feet mercilessly in an attempt to inflict as much pain as possible. They plied their trade with a drunken satanic fury until they were physically spent.

The last two butchers came forward with their hellish clawing flagellum laced with metal hooks and proceeded to flay the Sacred Body of their Lord and Master. The scourges fell forward again and again with all the fury of hell behind each and every blow cutting, ripping, tearing and shredding his Sacred Body into a bloody ghastly spectacle never before seen by human eyes. Pieces of his flesh fell to the ground to mix with the puddles of blood already there. As the whips continued to fall, Our Blessed Lord looked upon his two tormentors with blood filled eyes which begged for a little mercy but instead of relenting, they increased their savagery. Our Lord's feeble moans were now beginning to fade.

Just when it seems that Our Lord will be scourged to death a young man bolts past the Roman soldiers and screams at the lictors to stop before they kill a man who is not yet condemned. He came up so fast that it shocked the lictors and they stopped dead in their tracks. The young man then cut Our Lord's cords and disappeared back into the crowd. [137] Our Lord immediately slumped to the stone pavement and lay quivering in his own flesh, blood and vomit. For a few moments, no one

---

[137] It seems strange at first that the soldiers did not react to stop this man and that the lictors did not object. But at a second glance we see that Our Lord is not to die here but on the cross. The young man is thought to have been a relative of a blind man Our Lord had cured.

approached or bothered him. The lictors picked up their whips and rods and went back to the guard house.

During the whole time of the scourging Our Lord never ceased praying to the Eternal Father for the pardon of Our Sins. As he lay helpless on the blood spattered stones an Angel approached and gave him something to drink which restored some of his strength.

The bailiffs soon approached and ordered him to get dressed without the least intention of giving him any help. During the scourging his clothes had been purposely hidden so that he could suffer the indignity of being naked in front of the whole crowd for a longer period of time. They had been induced by Satan to do this to further try the patience of this man who knew well how to suffer.

The Holy Mother well understood the intentions of the hellish cohorts and was not about to allow it to happen. She ordered Satan and his demons to leave the area at once. They, being unable to resist her commands, fled immediately. She then ordered the Angels of her guard to bring Our Lord his clothes so that he could dress. When Our Lord came into possession of his garments his enemies chalked it up to more sorcery.

Our Lord was still lying at the base of the pillar in a state of shock. The cold morning air and the extreme sensitivity of his skin brought on by the blood sweating the night before in the garden had caused each and every blow to fill his body with untold suffering. As if all this wasn't enough, some of the bystanders now began to move in closer to the pillar. Some of them spit on him, insulted him and "kicked his sacred body about as if it had been a ball." [138]

Before he could make any attempt to rise and dress some of the executioners returned and began dragging him toward the sheep gate[139] which was nearby. They dragged him out of the

---

[138] Quote from the writings of Tertullian, an early church father.

[139] At this time it was the northern most gate of the city. It was at the end of the paved courtyard and was the same gate they went out to go to Herod's Palace.

gate for quite a distance to the Probatica (sheep) pool [140] and threw him into it to clean him up. They very roughly washed him up causing him an immense amount of pain as most of his body was raw meat. [141]

Then they brought him back to the pillar and ordered him once again to get dressed. He fumbled with his clothes as best he could but had a difficult time dressing with his bruised and swollen hands. The bailiffs became impatient and forced him to begin moving before he was fully dressed. He had to dress the rest of the way while fumbling with his clothes as he went. He wiped the blood from his eyes so that he could see his Mother as he passed by her. Her heart went out to him with all the motherly tenderness possible as he moved away from her, leaving his bloody footprints everywhere he stepped.

As he moved out of her sight into the forum a servant of Pilates' wife came up to her and handed her several large pieces of white linen which her mistress had provided. The Blessed Virgin used the linen, with the help of Magdalene to wipe all the Sacred Blood from off the pillar and the pavement.

Our Lord was brought into another large paved courtyard just to the north of and connected to the Fortress Antonio. This courtyard was surrounded on three sides by open hallways [142] and was completely open in the front which faced the forum. This courtyard was not open to the public and was only used by Roman soldiers. Within the courtyard was the guard house which housed a jail and served as a barracks for the executioners.

Some of the crowd tried to gather around the courtyard to see what was going to take place but were quickly displaced by the Roman cohort which moved them back into the Praetorium courtyard and surrounded the Antonio so that only they could see what was gong on.

---

[140] Also known as the pool of Bethesda.

[141] It is a possibility that all prisoners were washed in this manner after scourging.

[142] The outside of the hallways were a solid wall while the inside of the hallway was a series of columns which supported the roof but were open to the courtyard.

About fifty slaves and convicted criminals who served as executioners surrounded a broken column located in the middle of the courtyard which was short enough to serve as a stool. Even though Our Lord had just managed to get his clothes on as he arrived, they forced him to strip again and then sat him down on the make shift stool.

Some of their number had made a cap of thorns which they pressed down firmly on his forehead and then wrapped it around and over his head tying it tightly in the back to form a helmet of thorns. The sharp thorns dug into his entire scalp with many piercing down as far as his cheeks and even into his eyelids. [143] Using these thorns in mockery they crowned him king. They threw a purple robe over his shoulders and placed a reed into his hands to serve as a false scepter. Then Priests, Pharisees, bailiffs, executioners, Jew and pagan alike mocked and abused him. Kneeling down in false adoration they mocked and abused him all the more, spitting on him and striking his head with the reed which they tore from his grasp. They kicked punched and pulverized his body with all the glee of drunken sadists. Encouraged by the soldiers who were cheering and laughing, their torments followed every suggestion Satan and his cohorts could think of to test Our Lord's patience.

They relentlessly abused his body and pounded his head driving the thorns deep into the scalp until the blood flowed freely and filled his eyes and covered his face and beard.

Several times they viciously knocked him off the stool only to roughly place him on it again to continue their diabolical torments.

While the Roman cohort did not take physical part in the cruelty, their encouragement caused the tormentors to increase their efforts to please them as their audience. They did whatever they desired to do to him raising the cruelty of their torture to new and horrible heights.

---

[143] There are no words to describe the pain. The scalp is one of the most sensitive areas of the human body. For the most part this painful cap of thorns will be on his head until he dies.

At long last, Pilate sent word that Our Lord was to be brought back before him once again. The cohort pulled back into the forum and took up the positions they had been in before the crowning.

The Pharisees and Priests went back to their benches by the terrace but Our Lord was conducted into the fortress and up a set of stairs that led to a passageway which went into the Praetorium. They wished to avoid the massive crowd that was continuing to form. They stopped in an open portal at the edge of the terrace at a spot where Our Lord could not be seen by the crowd but was visible to the Governor.

Pilate could scarcely believe his eyes. Our Lord was battered beyond any point of recognition, even by him who had talked with him face to face only a short time ago. Even this unjust judge was moved by compassion for the person who now confronted him. Surely, Pilate thought, his enemies would now be satisfied and no longer demand his death. He walked to the portal where Our Lord stood and surveyed his condition even more closely.

Steadily throughout the morning the crowd had continued to grow until nearly all the inhabitants of the city were present, filling the paved courtyard and spilling over into the forum. Many clogged surrounding streets and even found perches on rooftops when the situation presented itself.

Pilate decided to bring Our Lord out onto the colonnade which surrounded the forum so that he could be seen by those in the courtyard and the forum. He ordered his soldiers to surround Our Lord and the bailiffs and to bring them out onto the colonnade to the point where it passed over the archway between the paved courtyard and the forum. From atop this archway Pilate could address the crowd in both the courtyard and the forum at the same time.

They stopped just short of the archway and Pilate went to a point just over it by himself. He called for silence and then addressed the crowd saying; "I bring him forth to you so that you may know that I find no cause in him. " Then he had the bailiffs bring Our Lord to where he was standing so that they were both in full view of the people. Our Lord was dressed only in the scant undergarment that hardly hid anything and the cape which they had used to mock him. Pilate raised the cape so that everyone could see the lictors handiwork. A collective gasp of horror went up from the crowd and they all just stood there in deathly silence. Such a sight as this had never been witnessed by a multitude in all of human history. Pilate turned him around so that all could see him from every side.

The people stood in stunned silence as they gazed upon his bruised, battered and mangled face. His nose was broken[144]and never before had they seen a man crowned with thorns which ripped into his scalp and covered his entire face with blood. His body was shredded and chards of flesh hung everywhere except where there was no flesh at all. In those places his bleached white bones were nauseatingly stained with his crimson blood. He shivered violently from the cold morning air, blunt trauma and high fever caused by severe dehydration and loss of blood. He teetered and shuddered, hardly able to maintain his balance. There was no intact skin visible anywhere and his entire body appeared to be one massive sickening red wound. [145]

Then Pilate said to the crowd in a loud clear voice; "Ecce Homo" (behold the man). [146]

At these words of the Governor the Blessed Virgin and her companions knelt down on the pavement and together with the Angels of her guard adored her Divine Son as the true God-man at this precise time when he was being exhibited as a spectacle before all the people. She prayed to the Eternal Father that Pilate would continue to maintain his innocence so that the entire world would know that he did not commit these crimes of which he was accused.

Looking out over the silent crowd Pilate felt that he had found the solution to his problem. Pointing to Our Lord he said to them; "what more can I do with him than to have punished

---

[144] Not his nose bone but the cartilage at the end of the nose.

[145] The only reason Our Lord is still alive at this point is because he wills it. At this point he has suffered beyond normal death many times.

[146] To this day this archway is referred to as the Ecce Homo arch.

him in this severe manner? You certainly have nothing more to fear from him! I do not find any cause of death in him."

He wrongly assumed that the mere sight of him would touch their hearts and inspire sympathy. He was wrong! Our Lord's enemies were far from satisfied. Our Lord may have been mangled, battered, bloodied, bruised and shredded into one massive wound but he wasn't dead.

At first the leaders began to complain and vent their hatred among themselves but being able to contain themselves no longer they shouted out in all their diabolical hatred which had only been increased by the sight of him; "Put him to death! Crucify him!" "Are you not content?" said Pilate, "The punishment he has received is beyond question sufficient to deprive him of all desire of making himself king." But they cried out even more until the cry spread throughout the entire multitude as if in one voice; "Crucify him! Crucify him!"

Pilate gazed at the crowd in utter disbelief and then turned his attention to his prisoner. Through the graces he had received from Our Blessed Lord and through the prayers offered for him by the Holy Mother, he felt compassion for Our Lord and was remorseful at the terrible punishment he had caused to be inflicted on him.

Then Pilate had the trumpets blown and raised his hands for silence. When the uproar had settled down he said to them; "take him yourselves and crucify him for I find no cause in him." Then the Priests said to Pilate; "we have a law and according to that law he ought to die because he made himself the Son of God." Pilate was immediately taken aback by this statement.

This is the first time that he has heard this charge. Is this why they really brought Our Lord to him? Is he claiming to be a Son of a God? Many times throughout the morning he had been highly impressed by his profound patience and the dignity of his bearing. Certainly their allegations that he was a dangerous criminal were not the least bit true. Their prior accusations had been contradictory and not the least believable but this new accusation that he claimed to be the Son of God was very unsettling to Pilate.

His wife once again sent a messenger out to him to remind him of his pledge not to condemn this just man. He sent her a return message that he would leave that decision in the hands of the Gods of Rome.

The Priests and the Pharisees had learned of the efforts of Pilates wife to intercede on behalf of Our Lord with her husband and caused rumors to circulate among the people that she had been won over by the friends of Our Lord and that he would be freed so that he could help the Romans destroy their city and put them to death.

Pilate did not like what he had just heard, even a little bit. Now he was more unsettled than before and was wracked with indecision. He was fearful of what he was dealing with and at this point simply did not know what to do. In frustration he again turned his attention to the enemies of Our Lord and said angrily; "I find no crime in him!" The leaders and the crowd went into an immediate uproar and shouted even louder than before, demanding that he be crucified.

Pilate turned abruptly away from them in complete disgust and started back to the Praetorium. He ordered that Our Lord be brought to him once again inside so that he could question him away from the screaming mob.

Once again Our Lord stood before Pilate in the great courtroom of the Romans. Pilate was in a terrible state. As far as he was concerned he had enough problems to deal with from Rome and those difficult to govern people milling around outside to get on the wrong side of a God. He was filled with fear and indecision. He was now plagued by the same doubts as Satan and his cohorts. How could the Son of a God allow himself to be treated in such a lowly manner? Human and satanic pride cannot accept such a concept. Was it possible, he asked himself, that this man standing in front of him barely recognizable as a human being could be the Son of a God?

"Where do you come from?" Pilate asked Our Lord. He received no answer. This time Pilate was put out by his silence and said angrily; "Will you not speak to me? Do you not know that I have the power to crucify you and I have the power to release you? With a great deal of effort Our Lord raised his weary, battered and tormented head and looking at Pilate through blood filled eyes said; "You would not have any power against me unless it were given to you from above; therefore, he that has delivered me to you has the greater sin." [147]

Pilate then adjured Our Lord to tell him if he was God; if he was the king promised to the Jews; where his kingdom was and to what class of Gods he belonged. Our Lord once again told him that his kingdom was not of this world. Then he pointed out to Pilate all his shortcomings and past misdeeds, warning him at the same time of the terrible fate which would befall him if he did not repent. Then he told him that on the final day he, Our Lord himself, would be his judge and pronounce a just judgment upon him.

Pilate was full of interior turmoil and was prey to many different emotions. His pride had been severely wounded in being suddenly confronted with all his own wrongdoing and it had made him terribly angry. At the same time he was scared out of his Roman wits by this man who knew his darkest secrets and who was warning him of the terrible consequences in store for him if he did not change his ways.

Pilate was thoroughly shaken and went back out onto the terrace more determined than ever to release his prisoner and he bluntly advised the leaders of Israel just that. But they were just as determined to see him put to death as Pilate was to set him free and suddenly became Roman patriots saying; "If you release this man you are not Caesars friend for whoever makes himself a king speaks against Caesar." Others yelled that they would make trouble for him with Caesar.

Pilate became sullen. He knew all to well that their threat was not an idle one as they had done just that in the past. He knew that what they said was true, that Tiberius would not allow anyone to call himself king without consent from Rome first. He

---

[147] Pilate was guilty of the same sin as Judas and the enemies of Our Lord but to a lesser degree. His enemies had not only acted out of hatred and envy but had failed to recognize him for who he was when they had all the means to do so. They had called him king, Messiah and Son of God while not believing it. They had ignored all his doctrines and miracles even though all of it was predicted by their own laws and Prophets.

had already earned the disfavor of Tiberius because of some of the actions he had taken in the past.

Then the cry went up again on all sides and seemingly from every corner of the Nation; "Crucify him! Crucify him!" The roar was absolutely deafening, so much so that Pilate began to fear an insurrection such as had taken place the year before at Passover time and he was most certain that Tiberius would not take kindly to another one. Unrest in the Roman Empire was never tolerated. It had now come down to a matter of two choices for Pilate, Our Lord's survival or his own. Pilate decided in favor of Pilate.

He called for a servant to bring him a basin of water and in the sight of all the people he washed his hands and declared loudly; "I am innocent of the blood of this just man. See to it yourselves." All the people answered; "His blood be upon us and upon our children."

Pilate then called for his judicial robes which were only used for official functions. After putting on his robes he placed a form of a crown on his head which was the symbol of his office as procurator. Then his servants placed a splendid looking mantle around his shoulders. He was now officially attired to carry out his duties as a judge of the Roman Empire.

Down in the paved courtyard there was an elevated platform used for rendering judgments which in Hebrew was called "Gabbatha". [148] Roman soldiers opened a path to this platform and Pilate, along with the officers of his tribunal and Roman Scribes descended the marble steps, passed through the crowd and ascended the steps of Gabbatha with Our Lord and the ever present bailiffs close behind. There was an official judgment seat on the platform in which Pilate seated himself. The officers gathered around him and the scribes took their places and made ready to record the entire event. Our Lord stood at the foot of the steps between two criminals who had been brought from the dungeon of the Fortress Antonio to be executed with him. These two had already been condemned at a prior date.

---

[148] A Hebrew word signifying an elevated place.

John was the only Apostle present at this proceeding. He, along with the holy women, stood with the Blessed Virgin. John and the women were in a terrible state of agitation but were comforted by the Most Holy Mother. She prayed to her Divine Son to console them in order that she may have their company until the end of this ordeal. Because of her intercession they were able to regain their composure.

Tears silently streamed down her face as she looked upon her Son about to be condemned. She offered all her torments and sufferings to the Eternal Father in union with those of her Divine Son. She appealed to the Angels of her guard to pray for friend and enemy alike for she knew more than anyone on earth the evil of sin and the mysteries of the redemption.

All the people of the city were now in the area or as close to these proceedings as they could get. [149] As soon as everyone was in place and all things were made ready, Pilate addressed the enemies of Our Lord and said; "behold your king!" But the cries of; "Crucify him! Crucify him!" Went up all around him. "Shall I crucify your king," said Pilate. The Priests replied; "We have no king but Caesar!" Seeing that once again things were beginning to get out of hand, Pilate began preparations to pass sentence on Our Lord.

The two crosses of the criminals flanking Our Lord had already been brought forward but Our Lord's cross was not yet present as he had yet to be officially condemned.

When Pilate was ready he had the trumpets sounded to demand silence. The Priests and their servants raised their hands in a gesture commanding silence from the people for they wanted the sentence read out loud in the presence of Our Lord and with all the people in attendance. When the crowd was finally silent, Pilate read the proclamation.

---

[149] The Jewish historian Flavius Josephus states that at this particular time in history the population of Jerusalem was about seven hundred thousand but with the influx of people from all over the nation and the Mediterranean basin for the Passover festival it had swelled to about one million, seven hundred thousand.

"I Pontius Pilate, presiding over lower Galilee and governing Jerusalem in loyalty to the Roman Empire and being within the executive mansion, judge, decide and proclaim that I condemn to death Jesus of the Nazarene people and a Galilean by birth, a man opposed to our laws, to our senate and the great Emperor Tiberius Caesar. For the execution of this sentence I decree that his death be upon the cross and he shall be fastened thereto with nails as is customary with criminals because in this very place, gathering around himself every day men, poor and rich, he has continued to raise tumults throughout Judea, proclaiming himself the Son of God and king of Israel at the same time threatening ruin of this renowned city of Jerusalem and its Temple and of the sacred empire, refusing to give tribute to Caesar and because he dared to enter into triumph, this city of Jerusalem and the Temple of Solomon accompanied by a great multitude of the people carrying branches of palms. [150] I command the first Centurion Quintus Cornelius to lead him for his greater shame through the said city of Jerusalem bound as he is and scourged by my orders. [151] Let him also wear his own garments that he may be known to all and let him carry the cross on which he is to be crucified. Let him walk through all the public streets between two other thieves who are likewise condemned to death for their robberies and murders so that this punishment be an example to all the people and all the malefactors. I desire also and command in this my sentence that this malefactor having been led through the public streets be brought outside the city through the Pagora Gate, now called the Antonio Portal [152] and under the proclamation of the herald who shall mention all the crimes pointed out in my proclamation, he shall be conducted to the summit of the mountain called Calvary where justice is to be executed upon the wicked transgressors. There fastened and crucified upon the cross, which shall be

---

[150] Every bit of it is untrue except for the Palm Sunday procession.
[151] This confirms the presence of the first cohort in Jerusalem as the first centurion or the "primus pilus" was the highest ranking combat officer in the legion and was always the Centurion of the first century of the first cohort.
[152] Know to the Jews as the Garden Gate.

carried as decreed above, his body shall remain between the aforesaid thieves. Above the cross, that is at its top, he shall have placed for him his name and title in three languages, namely; Hebrew, Greek and Latin and in all and each one of them shall be written; "This is Jesus of Nazareth; King of the Jews", so that it may be understood by all and universally known. At the same time I command that no one, no matter of what condition, under pain of loss of his goods and his life and under a punishment of rebellion against the Roman Empire presume audaciously to impede the execution of this just sentence. Ordered by me to be executed with all the rigor according to the decrees and laws of the Romans and Hebrews. [153]

Pilate then took a long stick into his hands, broke it and threw the fragments down at the feet of Our Lord. He then wrote down his sentence in the official Roman record but he did not write what he had just proclaimed. Instead he wrote; "I have been compelled, for fear of an insurrection, to yield to the wishes of the High Priests, the Sanhedrin and the people who tumultuously demanded the death of Jesus of Nazareth whom they accused of having disturbed the public peace and for also having blasphemed and broken their laws. I have given him up to them to be crucified although their accusations appeared to be groundless. I have done so for fear of their alleging to the Emperor that I encouraged insurrection and cause dissatisfaction among the Jews by denying them the rights of justice." [154] The Roman scribes then made copies.

Pilate then wrote the large inscription to be placed on the cross and ordered his scribes to make several copies to be distributed throughout the country for display. The High Priests were extremely upset at what he had written and argued with Pilate that it should read; "He said I am King of the Jews, not

---

[153] This proclamation was probably written by Pilate's scribes in unison with some Jewish scribes as it contains much legalese and refers to both Jewish and Roman Law. The wording of the sign and inscription are at the insistence of Pilate. Proclamation quote is from the Mystical City of God by Mary of Agreda.

[154] Quote from the Dolorous Passion of Our Lord Jesus Christ by Anne Catherine Emmerich.

simply King of the Jews". Pilate was also highly irritated and snapped back; "what I have written, I have written!"

Our Lord's enemies also argued that they wanted his cross to be lower than the two thieves as they wished to humiliate him even more. Knowing that his cross would have to be made higher to support the inscription they tried to get Pilate not to display it at all but just as they would not listen to reason regarding the innocence of Our Lord, Pilate would not listen to any of their requests. The inscription would be put into place just as he had written it.

It was over and done with. There was no more to be said. Our Lord was given over to the bailiffs who immediately ripped off his purple cape and gave him his own clothes to put on. Not being able to put on his robe over the crown of thorns they brutally ripped it off his head opening many news wounds.

As soon as he was dressed he was reshackled and rebound with ropes and chains.

He was then forced to stand between the two thieves who were also bound, to await his cross. Both thieves were riddled with black and blue marks from the prior day's scourging but their bodies looked nothing like Our Lord's.

One thief stood quietly while the other reviled and abused Our Lord along with the bailiffs. Our Lord looked upon his new companions with loving compassion and prayed for them but as he looked out over this people who had clamored for his death, his very own people, his heart and soul was filled to overflowing with grief. [155]

---

[155] Father P. Gallway, S.J. in his book "The Watches of the Passion" says; "Even his own Blessed Mother cannot mourn over the death of her only Son as he mourns over the loss of his people. To his loving heart the loss of his people is as great as the sea.

Chapter V
The Carrying of the Cross

As soon as the sentence was proclaimed the greater part of those assembled in the forum and paved courtyard began to trickle away. Some went back to their homes and others to the Temple to prepare for the Passover. A great number of them hurried to get to the place of execution ahead of the procession to get a good spot to watch from. Still others stayed right where they were so they could follow the procession.

Pilate left the judgment platform with his guards, crossed the paved courtyard and went up the Scala Santa onto the terrace. He stopped for a moment and looked at the scene unfolding before him in the courtyard below. Then he turned abruptly and went into the Praetorium.

A large number of Roman soldiers formed skirmish lines in front of the Praetorium and stood at the ready to ward off any kind of trouble which might develop but what was left of the crowd seemed more curious than prone to violence.

A large number of Pharisees on horseback came into the forum with the intention of accompanying the procession to Calvary. Among them were the six political enemies of Our Lord who had been present in the Garden of Olives when he was arrested and brutally shackled.

Some of the executioners lifted up the cross beams for the crosses of the two thieves and laid them across their backs from shoulder to shoulder. They forced them to put their arms up and over the beams to hold them up and then tied their hands securely to the beams. The upright beams to their crosses were to be carried by slaves who accompanied the executioners.

The Bailiffs forced Our Lord to move to the middle of the courtyard where the executioners were waiting with his cross. The upright beam of his cross was about fifteen feet long and the two cross beams were tied securely to it. Unlike the two thieves who were only going to carry their cross beams Our Lord was being made to carry the entire cross which was altogether larger than either of theirs. As he was led up to them they threw it down at his feet.

Our Lord kneeled down beside his cross and then to the astonishment of all hugged it and kissed it saying; "Oh cross, beloved of my soul, now prepared and ready to still my longings, come to me that I may be received into your arms and that attached to you as on an altar I may be accepted by the Eternal Father as the sacrifice of his everlasting reconciliation with the human race. In order to die upon you I have descended from Heaven and assumed mortal and passive flesh for you are to be the scepter with which I will triumph over all my enemies; the key with which I will open the gates of Heaven for all the predestined, the sanctuary in which the guilty sons of Adam will find mercy and the treasure house for the enrichment of their poverty. Upon you, I wish to exalt and recommend dishonor and reproach among men in order that my friends may embrace them with joy, seek them with anxious longings and follow me on the path which I, through you, will open for them."

He then addressed his Heavenly Father saying; "My Father and Eternal God, I confess you as the Lord of Heaven and Earth, subjecting myself to your power and to your Divine wishes. I take upon my shoulders the wood for the sacrifice of my innocent and passive humanity and I accept it willingly for the salvation of men. Receive, Eternal Father, this sacrifice as acceptable to your justice in order that from today on they may no longer be servants but sons and heirs of your kingdom with me." [156]

Although his Holy Mother could not physically see what was happening to her Divine Son at that particular moment, all was shown to her by the Eternal Father. She immediately understood the infinite value of the cross the very moment that Our Lord touched it. She too adored and venerated it at the same time that he was kissing and adoring it. She imitated her most holy Son in every token of affection with which he received the

---

[156] Quote from the Mystical City of God by Mary of Agreda.

136

altar of wood on which he would be sacrificed to atone for the sins of men.

The Bailiffs then picked up the cross and placed in on his right shoulder while he was still kneeling on the ground.

Satan was watching very closely all that was taking place. He and his cohorts still could not believe that a God-Man could be the brunt of all the humiliation with which this man allowed himself to be subject to but when the cross was placed on his shoulder they were suddenly beset with new fears and confusion. Satan himself was seized with a dread that somehow the suffering and death of this man was going to cause serious destruction to his reign and designs. He and his companions decided to leave this place and these circumstances which made them so uncomfortable and return quickly to the caverns of Hell.

The Eternal Father informed the Blessed Virgin of their plans to flee and giving her power over them instructed her on what to do. She immediately turned toward the demons and forbid them to flee. She ordered them to remain and witness all the events of the passion which were about to begin and to remain in attendance until the very end on Mount Calvary. Though they tried with all their might the demons could not resist the great power at work in this holiest of all women.

One hundred Roman soldiers came from the forum into the courtyard to act as an escort for the procession. [157]

Pilate emerged from the Praetorium in full combat armor. A trumpet was sounded signifying that it was time for the procession to begin its movement toward Calvary.

The four bailiffs had once again tied ropes to his waist belt so that they could pull him front or back as they had been doing all day. Two more bailiffs entered the fray by tying ropes to the bottom of the cross so that they could hold it up so as not to let it drag on the ground, forcing him to carry most of its weight.

---

[157] The main purpose of this detachment of soldiers is to conduct the procession to Calvary without any interference. Although they are in full combat gear, they carry no whips or implements of execution. That is the work of slaves and executioners, not soldiers.

The Centurion Quintus Cornelius who commanded the century assigned to escort, gave the order to begin moving. One of the Pharisees came up to Our Lord and said: "Rise! We have had a sufficiency of the fine speeches; Rise and set off."[158]

Our Lord found it very difficult to get up on his own bearing the weight of the cross and they roughly jerked him up until he was standing on his feet. His entire body shuddered and trembled under the massive weight and it seemed as if he would tumble to the ground at any moment.

A herald led the procession. It was his job to sound his trumpet and recite the names, charges and type of sentence each criminal was under each time he came to an intersection or any other gathering of people.

Next came a portion of the Roman escort followed by slaves who were mostly women and children carrying the smaller implements of crucifixion such as nails, ropes, tools and baskets filled with other odds and ends. Male slaves followed them carrying the larger implements for crucifixion such as ladders and the upright beams for the crosses. Then came some of the Pharisees on horseback and behind them a young boy who carried Pilate's inscription and the crown of thorns.

Behind this young boy came Our Lord struggling to take each step, bearing his heavy cross on his mutilated shoulder. His bruised and swollen bare feet screamed with pain each time he set them down upon the very earth which he himself had created, not in just his attempts to move forward but also just to maintain his balance and remain upright. His exhausted body which was completely covered with open bloody oozing wounds had not had the benefit of sleep, food or drink since the supper Thursday evening, was thoroughly weakened from blood loss, thirst, hunger, fever and pain.

Holding onto the cross with his right hand as best he can he often has to struggle with his left hand to attempt to pull up his long garment which he keeps stepping on with his bloody feet. Again the two bailiffs in front of him tug him forward while

---

[158] Quote from the Dolorous Passion of Our Lord Jesus Christ by Anne Catherine Emmerich.

the two behind tug backwards making it difficult for him to stay on his feet.

For these tormentors of his he prays constantly. In return for his kindness he receives abuse, insults, curses, blasphemies and blows. Subject to the power of his Most Holy Mother, Satan and his cohorts followed after him as if they too were bound with chains and ropes. [159]

Behind Our Lord came the two thieves carrying their cross beams. One of them was calm and silent while the other was constantly angry and kept cursing and swearing as they went along. Then came more Pharisees on horseback followed by the rest of the Roman soldiers. Roman soldiers also covered each flank of the procession

What was left of the curious mob followed the procession behind the last contingent of Romans.

The procession moved slowly to the west, passed behind the Fortress Antonio then turned abruptly south. Moving past the western wall of the great fort they entered Jerusalem through the Antonio gate. Once into the city the herald began at once to make his proclamations.

When the Blessed Virgin heard these pronouncements, she, together with the Holy Angels of her guard, composed songs of praise and worship regarding the innocence of her Most Holy Son. They offered these sweet canticles to the Eternal Father while all Jerusalem seemed to be filling the air with blasphemies.

She alone at the present time understood all the deep mysteries of the redemption which Our Lord was accomplishing through the actions of his persecutors. She was the only one who knew the importance connected to his passion and death. She remained completely faithful in suffering with him and imitating his example. She never allowed herself the slightest comfort; no sleep, no drink or food and no rest. She continually experienced in her own body all that her Divine Son was suffering.

---

[159] God imposed this punishment on Satan and his followers because of the evil committed by him in bringing sin and death into the world. He was now forced to witness the remedy to his wrongdoing.

Pilate was taking no chances that civil unrest might develop along the way of the cross. The mood of the crowd in and around the forum and courtyard had been ugly. He ordered a squadron of cavalry to fall in behind the mob which was following the procession. Then he joined the procession surrounded by many of his officers as they followed the cavalry unit. Behind Pilate and his officers came another three hundred Roman foot soldiers in full combat array.

After entering the city, the road which ran south along the western wall of the Temple began to slope steeply downward into the Thyropian Valley. [160] When they reached the Temple gate they turned westward onto a street that was somewhat wider but still very steep. Our Lord struggled with every step just to keep his balance. The heavy cross was crushing his mangled shoulder and together with the terrible pains in his feet was almost maddening. Due to the roughness of the street, the rapid decline and the constant tugging on the ropes by the morbid bailiffs each step was an agony.

The street they had entered was not a main thoroughfare and was chosen by the Roman escort for the purpose of crowd control. Once they entered this street the soldiers no longer allowed the members of the mob to follow them. The street narrowed as they continued their downward journey forcing them all closer together which allowed the bailiffs an opportunity to torment him all the more.

Once at the bottom of the street they had entered into the Thyropian Valley and the lower part of the city. An underground Aqueduct which flowed down into the valley from atop Mount Zion ran through this part of the city and went under the road which the procession was on. A large flat stone had been laid across the waterway to act as a makeshift bridge. As Our Lord stepped up onto the bridge he stumbled and fell with the cross crashing to the road beside him.

The procession ground to a halt which infuriated the bailiffs who abused and beat him without mercy for causing this

---

[160] Also know as the valley of the cheese makers, it ran the entire length of the city from north to south.

delay. Being too weak to get up on his own, Our Lord held out his hand for someone to help him but instead they abused him all the more. He prayed for those who would not even give a little help or pity and receiving a little strength from on high managed to raise his head. When the bailiffs saw this they used the occasion to snatch the crown of thorns away from the boy who carried it and cruelly jammed it back onto his head in order to increase his torments.

One of the Pharisees ordered them to lift him up fearing that he would die in their hands and not make it to the cross. Responding to this command the bailiffs pulled him to his feet and as soon as he was standing erect put the cross back upon his right shoulder. The addition of the crown of thorns forced him to tilt his head sharply to the left. Once again they were on the move and due to the unsteadiness of his movements the cross bumped against the crown driving the thorns deep into his flesh with agonizing pain.

The bailiffs constantly pulled and pushed Our Savior with inhuman cruelty causing him to struggle constantly to keep his balance but he failed to do so many times and went crashing to the street opening gaping wounds on his knees and shoulder. Each time he fell they severely mistreated him as if each fall had been designed by him to purposely cause delays.

Once across the Thyropian Valley it was uphill all the rest of the way. The streets consist of mostly steps and small terraces. Horses, donkeys and camels could go up these streets but not any wheeled vehicles.

As Our Lord struggles up each step under the brutal weight of the cross people curse, jeer and verbally abuse him from windows, doorways and roof tops. They toss small stones and other debris into the street which cause untold pain to his already battered, swollen and bruised feet as he steps on them. Those who can get close enough cover him with spit and throw dirt from the street into his face partially blinding the eyes that look upon them with such mercy and compassion.

He can barely move but they still try to hasten his steps as they are so anxious to see him die. They never give him a chance to catch his breath and are totally oblivious to the fact that because of their brutal actions he should by all rights already be dead. By this time they are so filled with hate, rage and demonic fury that they are devoid of all human compassion, mercy and the light of any grace.

Pilate, with his cavalry and troops does not follow the procession through these same narrow streets but goes a little further south to a main street and uses a parallel route. His intention is to keep people away from the procession and to prevent any form of insurrection which might develop.

Due to the fact that the crowds and soldiers were clogging the streets and the escorts were keeping people back away from the procession The Blessed Virgin was not able to get anywhere near her Divine Son. She petitioned the Eternal Father for permission to be near her Son and to be at the foot of the cross when he died. In light of this fact she ordered the Angels of her guard to clear a path to her Divine Son and at the same time made her wishes known to John.

John then led the Blessed Virgin into the Thyropian Valley by another route while the Angels cleared the way before them. The Angels inspired John to bring Our Lady to a large house along the way which was owned by Ciaphas whose servants John seemed to know well. [161] This house had a front door on the main street Pilate was on and the back door opened to the street the procession was on.

A servant answered the door and after a short conversation allowed them to go through the house to the back. John and the Holy Mother stood in the doorway. All the mean, insulting and outrageous language which was turning the Jerusalem air blue with curses and blasphemies fell upon her saintly ears. Through it all she could hear the herald announcing the crimes and sentences of the condemned walking behind him and she could make out the procession slowly laboring up the street as it approached the spot where she stood.

She fell to her knees and prayed fervently for strength. Then they stood silently watching the painfully slow procession as it advanced towards them. The slaves who were carrying the

---

[161] Again that mysterious connection of John to the High Priests.

instruments of execution began to pass by them. And when she spotted the instruments of execution her motherly instincts overwhelmed her emotions and she joined her hands in prayer and petitioned Heaven for assistance.

The executioners inquired as to whom this woman was who was uttering such lamentations and when told that she was his mother, they thrust the nails of execution under her nose instead of being moved sympathetically and made fun of her.

She simply turned her head away from them to look at her Divine Son who was now getting close to her. His face was red with blood from the miserable crown and the weight of the cross twisted and contorted his body as he struggled forward. He raised his head and looked at her with deep love and compassion, then stumbled and fell. She rushed forward and knelt by his side and threw her arms around him. They did not speak nor did the bailiffs allow her time to speak. No one dared touch her but the bailiffs rebuked her saying; "What have you to do here woman? He would not have been in our hands if he had been brought up better." [162]

John and a few of the holy women came into the street to help raise her up. Some of the Roman soldiers appeared touched by her actions but ordered her to return to the doorway. She immediately obeyed them.

She prayed interiorly to her Divine Son [163] who was so heavily burden with the immense weight of his cross. Since she could not herself take the cross from him and since he would not allow her to order her Holy Angels to make it lighter she prayed that he would inspire his tormentors to get some one to help him saying; "My Son and Eternal God, light of my eyes and light of my soul, receive Oh Lord the sacrifice of my not being able to relieve you of the burden of the cross and carry it myself who am a daughter of Adam; for it is I who should die upon it in love of you as you now wish to die in most ardent love of the human

---

[162] Quote from the Dolorous Passion of Our Lord Jesus Christ by Anne Catherine Emmerich.
[163] She still carried him interiorly in her bosom in the Blessed Sacrament according to his wishes and designs.

race. Oh most loving mediator between guilt and justice, how do you cherish mercy in the midst of so great injuries and such heinous offences? Oh love without measure or bounds which permits such torments and affronts in order to afford it a wider scope for it eagerness and effectiveness. Oh infinite and sweetest love I wish that the hearts and wills of men were all mine so that they could give no such thankless return for all that you endure. Oh who will speak to the hearts of mortals to teach them what they owe you since you have paid so dearly for their salvation from ruin. " [164]

The bailiffs raised Our Lord back up to his feet and returned the cross to his shoulder. Again the procession renewed its woeful climb toward Calvary. They soon came to an intersection of three streets that converged on a small square. Our Lord fell again and this time remained motionless and unable to get up no matter what they did to him.

He had heard his mother's prayer for someone to help him and now granted her request. The Pharisees addressed the Roman soldiers and asked them to find someone to help him carry his cross as in his condition he might not make it to Calvary alive. [165]

A man accompanied by three children happened to enter the square on his way home and had every intention of passing them by. The soldiers seeing by his manner of dress that he was a pagan stopped him and ordered him to help Our Lord with his cross. [166]

At first he objected profusely but soon realized that he was not going to get out of it. His children were upset and scared but some nearby women quieted them down and took charge of

---

[164] Quote from the Mystical City of God by Mary of Agreda.

[165] The reason they address this request to the Romans is that under the legal agreement between the Romans and the Jews, the Romans could press someone into service for a reasonable time or distance when a need arose. This had prompted the teaching of Our Lord; "If a man press you into service for a mile, go with him two."

[166] It shows some sensitivity by the Romans to Jewish custom as a pagan would not be defiled by carrying the cross.

them.[167] The first reaction of Simon was one of anger at being made to walk with a man in such terrible condition. His busy day was being interrupted and his children were being scared out of their wits at seeing their father seized by Roman soldiers. Although he was ready to comply with the instructions of the soldiers he verbally expressed his great annoyance at being inconvenienced in this manner. Then he glanced down at the man who was the cause of all his trouble and the man looked directly at him. Simon saw the tears mingled with blood cutting furrows down his battered face and those eyes looked upon him with such love and compassion that he stopped complaining immediately. Any reluctance he had entertained completely melted away and he reached down and helped Our Lord to his feet.

The bailiffs untied the two cross pieces from the upright beam and gave part of the cross to Simon to carry [168] behind Our Lord reducing his burden. They had not gone far before Simon under went a complete transformation in the order of grace. [169]

When they had made their way upward about two hundred steps from where Simon had been pressed into service a stately looking woman, holding her young daughter by the hand, came out of a well to do home on the left side of the street. The

---

[167] His name was Simon and he had come to live in Jerusalem from a city in Libya. He was a gardener by trade. His two older sons were Alexander and Rufus who later on became Disciples. History does not record the name of the youngest son.

[168] There is no reference made as to who carried what part of the cross. It is reasonable to assume that Simon was given either one or both of the arm pieces and Our Lord continued to carry and drag the long upright piece. The ropes to hold the end up off the ground were removed.

[169] To this point Our Lord has suffered every aspect of the passion unaided except for the passive suffering of his Mother in union with his sufferings and sorrows. Now he allows Simon to suffer with him, actively, for awhile, to show the rest of us that while he alone can bring about infinite atonement for our sins we are not freed from offering finite atonement for our sins. We too must suffer for our sins. "If any man would come after me, let him deny himself and take up his cross and follow me."(Matthew Chap: 2 Vs 24). Atonement for sin continues in the Mystical body of Christ (the church) prompting St Paul to say; "I rejoice in my sufferings for your sake and in my flesh I am filling up what is lacking in the afflictions of Christ on behalf of his body, The Church. (Colossians Chap: I, Vs 24-25). This applies to us also.

young girl was clutching a goblet of wine in her hand that was free. They walked boldly past the soldiers and straight up to Our Lord without interference from anyone. The woman fell on her knees before her Master and held out a veil to him saying; "Permit me to wipe the face of Our Lord." [170] He took the veil in his left hand, wiped his face and returned it to her with gratitude. She kissed it and put it under her outer garment so no one would take it. The little girl sheepishly offered Our Lord the goblet of wine but by this time the bailiffs had recovered from their initial shock at the boldness of these two and would not allow him to drink it; then commanded these brash females to go back into their house.

The Pharisees and bailiffs were infuriated by this act of veneration shown to Our Lord at a time when they were trying to present him to the Jewish people as a low life criminal. To appease their anger they lashed out at Our Lord and struck him repeatedly.

The woman and her daughter went quickly back into their house. She took the veil out from under her cloak and spread it out on a table then she and her daughter fell on their knees to pray. [171] A short time later a friend entered the room and noticed the bloody imprint of Our Lord's face on the veil. [172]

Once again the procession got underway amid curses and shouts while the physical abuse, insults and abominations continued in full force. Slowly but steadily they moved up the

---

[170] Quote from the Dolorous Passion of Our Lord Jesus Christ by Anne Catherine Emmerich.

[171] This woman's name was Seraphia and she was the wife of a high ranking Temple official named Sirach. She was also a cousin of John the Baptist as Zachariah and her father were brothers. She was also related to the Herod family on her husband's side. In tradition she is believed to be the same woman Our Lord cured of a long time hemorrhage.

[172] Because of this imprint, Seraphia would come to be known by the name of Veronica (Vera Icon meaning true portrait). She eventually placed the veil in the hands of the Blessed Virgin who in turn left it to the Apostles. The Apostles put the veil into the hands of the Church where it remains to this day. The veil had three folds and the image was on all three. The images are preserved in three places; Spain, Jerusalem and Rome. When this image is compared to the image on the shroud of Turin they are found to be identical.

street toward the western wall of the great city. As they reached more level ground on the approach to the gate the bailiffs spotted a pool of putrid scummy water and purposely shoved him into it. There were evil sinister grins as howls of laughter pierced the morning air from his gleeful enemies while the soldiers looked on with complete indifference.

As Our Lord lay in the filthy water near the city gate he repeated his lamentation over his beloved Jerusalem saying; "Jerusalem, Jerusalem, how often would I have gathered together your children as the hen gathers her chicks under her wings; but you would not." The Pharisees in particular were enraged by his words by which he seemed to lay claim to the people of their fair city. More brutal beatings and insults were heaped upon him as they ordered him to get back up and to get on the move again.

Fed up with the awful treatment he was forced to witness, Simon yelled at his handlers that if they continued their brutal conduct he would throw down the cross and not carry it any further even if they killed him. They looked at him with eyes full of contempt but stopped their punishment partly because of his tirade and partly because it was getting late.

The procession moved beyond the western wall, passing through the garden gate. [173] Calvary was located directly to the north of the gate at a distance of about four hundred yards with its back bank only about forty yards away from the city wall.

About one hundred yards from the base of Calvary they reached an intersection where many women and their children were gathered together crying and uttering lamentations. When they saw Our Lord's mutilated condition close up they began to wail all the more.

Our Lord stopped and seeing that he could hardly stand, Simon rushed to his aid to help him keep his balance. Looking at these women with great compassion he said to them; "Daughters of Jerusalem. Do not weep for me but weep for yourselves and your children. For behold the days are coming when they will say blessed are the barren and the wombs that never bore and the

---

[173] So called because of the beautiful gardens which existed just outside the gate even to the base of Calvary.

breasts that never nursed. Then they will say to the mountains, fall on us and to the hills; cover us. For if they do this when the wood is green, what will happen when it is dry?" [174]

During the time that Our Lord had been addressing the women the executioners had gone on ahead to Calvary with all their implements. Pilate and his troops had stopped just inside the gate as he had no intention of taking the entire unit outside the city. He ordered one of the centuries with him to go on ahead and secure Calvary and its surrounding area. When he was satisfied that all was in order and that no insurrection was imminent he turned his troops around and started back to the Roman compound. [175]

When Our Lord finished addressing the women the procession moved on. There were five different paths leading up to the summit of Calvary. The paths to the south and west went up gradual inclines and provided easy access. The path on the east side of the plateau between the city and the mount was steep and rough. They led him toward this path. At the foot of Calvary he crashed to the ground harder than he had at any of his previous falls with the cross slamming down on top of him. The bailiffs treated him with more cruelty after this fall then they had after any of the others. They kicked, pummeled, cursed and insulted him with all the fury of a savage beast before they got him back up to his feet.

After all this they forced him up the steep rough path carrying the upright beam amidst more curses, insults beatings and lashings than would be heaped upon a despised animal being

---

[174] These women are distraught at his great sufferings. With deep compassion he stopped and acknowledged their concern. Then he gently told them that they should not be weeping over his torments but over their sins which were causing his torments. For if sin is causing him, who is without sin and incapable of sin(green wood) to suffer such torments what will happen to those who are guilty of sin (dry wood) on the day of judgment. Because of their concern for him they were given the grace to understand what he said. The others present were not.

[175] There were now two hundred Roman soldiers and their officer on and in the immediate vicinity of Calvary. The one hundred he had sent to secure the mount and the one hundred who had escorted the procession.

led to slaughter. When he reached the summit he dropped the beam and slumped limply to the ground.

By this time Simon was not only exhausted but completely fed up. He was teetering on the point of rage and insisted on staying so that he could continue to assist Our Lord further. The bailiffs made fun of his desire to help and drove him away. At the same time the executioners dismissed the slaves who had carried the implements and sent them back to the guard house at Antonio.

The Pharisees who had gone around to the western side of Calvary to bring their horses up the gradual slope now arrived on the summit. [176] The two thieves were not brought to the top right away but were made to lie on the ground at the foot of the mount under Roman guard.

The executioners laid the three pieces of the cross on the ground where they intended to assemble it. They came to Our Lord and dragged him by the ropes that were still attached to his waist belt and threw him on the ground beside the cross, telling the most powerful king that they were about to prepare his throne. He crawled onto the cross under his own power and stretched out his limbs so that they could make their measurements. While the executioners did their preparatory work many of the Pharisees mingled around the cross and offered many insulting remarks. When they were finished, the executioners dragged him to a cave used for a holding cell, locked him in stocks to prevent any escape and closed the door.

After meeting her son in the street John took the Blessed Virgin and her companions into the lower city to a house owned by Lazarus. They spent a little time there weeping and mourning. After a short time they went back out into the city and began once again to retrace the steps of Our Lord while the Holy Mother pointed out to them the places most consecrated by

---

[176] Calvary could hardly be classified as a mountain. It was more like a Mesa or a plateau. Its highest point was its back side near the city wall which rose to about twenty feet. Its surface was about sixty feet long by forty five feet wide or about twenty seven hundred square feet. It is called Calvary or Golgotha which means skull because of a tradition that states that one of the sons of Noah buried the skull of Adam here.

particular sufferings her Divine Son had undergone. When they neared the vicinity of the house of Seraphia on the way to Calvary they encountered Pilate and his troops. To clear the street and make room for the soldiers they entered the home of Seraphia. When she showed them the veil she had presented to Our Lord they were filled with joy at the miraculous sight and revered it with great humility. They continued on their way to Calvary praising, rejoicing and thanking God for the gift of this precious relic.

On the summit of Calvary the executioners dug out the three holes that would be needed for the placement of the crosses. They then brought Our Lords cross quite near to the spot where they had dug the hole and planned to erect it. They fastened the two arms to the main beam and then nailed a block of wood to the beam for a foot rest.

The Blessed Virgin and her companions reached the bottom of Calvary at the western slope. Many of the holy women chose to remain there while a few more went up about half way. John, The Blessed Virgin, Mary Heli, Mary Cleophus and Mary Magdalene went all the way to the summit. No one interfered with them; Not Pharisees, soldiers, bailiffs or executioners for the Holy Mother had obtained this privilege from the Eternal Father for all of them to be close to her Divine Son until he died on the cross.

The Pharisees rode their horses back and forth among the people while the executioners went about their work getting everything ready for the execution. The Roman soldiers kept their silent watch, ever vigilant for any sign of trouble or interference.

The Holy Mother was suffering deeply at not being able to be near or even see her suffering Son. Her eyes kept coming back to that cross lying on the ground, its arms outstretched waiting for her Divine Son to ascend and sanctify it. She looked at the hammers, ropes, nails and all the instruments of torture which lay on the ground near the executioners who were busy with final preparations. They cursed and swore as they went about their work while she prayed and offered acts of reparation. She thought about all that he had already suffered for the love of the human race and contemplated all that he would still suffer before it would all come to an end.

Hail had fallen several times during the course of the morning but now the sun was fully out and the sky had completely cleared. It was now getting close to the noon hour and the crowd, soldiers and the enemies of Our Lord began to murmur among themselves and to point out and discuss something that they had never seen before. A thick fog began to rise all around them reducing the range of vision. What caused all the uneasiness was that the fog was red in color. Who in this world had ever seen such a phenomenon as red fog? As it rose over this place of abomination the light from the sun took on a strange dullness and began to dim.

Chapter VI
The Crucifixion

When they had finished preparing the cross, four of the bailiffs went to the holding cell and brought Our Lord out. He was greeted with a hail of abusive language from many of the bystanders. The Roman soldiers were as yet indifferent to the proceedings but watched the action of the crowd very closely for any signs of violent behavior.

Some of the holy women half way down the slope gave money to a man standing nearby to take a goblet of sweet wine that Seraphia had brought up to the summit and bribe the bailiffs to let him drink it. He did as they asked but the executioners took it and drank it themselves. [177]

Demons were everywhere on Calvary and even though they could not leave there was no prohibition placed on their normal methods of reeking havoc. They were urging and exciting the executioners to use greater cruelty than they would have thought of on their own. They also incited the bystanders to revile, jeer and insult Our Lord. They were hard at work tempting all that were disposed to listen to their evil suggestions.

Angels were also present in great numbers. Although they were not allowed to give assistance to their Lord and God except in rare cases when he let them, they tried as best they could to comfort, console and give courage to those who were favorable to him.

Even though the chief Priests wanted to keep themselves from taking the blame for putting him to death by placing the blame on the Romans, they couldn't resist sticking their noses

---

[177] There were many bailiffs and executioners on Calvary. Those who scourged him; those who had been with him since the garden; those who had held the ropes on the cross as well as the many executioners who were present to crucify all the condemned. Some were employed by the Priests and some were employed by or were slaves of the Romans. All were pagans and not obliged to keep Jewish Law. It is logical to assume that those employed by the Romans were more adept at crucifixion than those employed by the Priests.

into the proceedings and barking directions and orders instead of keeping themselves at a reasonable distance.

The cross was lying on the ground just a short distance from where it was to be erected and the bailiffs brought Our Lord up to it.

Seeing that her Divine Son was about to be stripped of his clothes and crucified, the Holy Mother prayed interiorly to the Eternal Father; "My Lord and Eternal God you are the Father of your only begotten Son. By eternal generation he is engendered God of the true god, namely yourself and as man he was born of my womb and received from me this human nature in which he is now suffering. I have nursed and sustained him at my own breast and as the best of sons that can ever be born of any creature; I love him with maternal love. As his Mother I have a natural right in the person of his most holy humanity and your providence will never infringe upon any rights held by your creatures. This right of a Mother then, I now yield to you and once more place in your hands your and my Son as a sacrifice for the redemption of man. Accept, my Lord, this pleasing offering since this is more than I can ever offer by submitting my own self as a victim or to suffering. This sacrifice is greater not only because my Son is the true God and of your own substance but because this sacrifice causes me a much greater sorrow and pain. For if the lots were changed and I should be permitted to die in order to preserve his most holy life I would consider it a great relief and the fulfillment of my dearest wishes." [178]

When she finished her prayer she noticed that the executioners were preparing a bitter drink of wine mixed with myrrh and gall. It was the custom to mix wine with myrrh to give to the condemned to somewhat dull the pain but not gall. They were only adding the bitter gall to torment his sense of taste and make him thirst all the more. It was a rotten sadistic thing to do and she asked her Divine Son not to drink it. He did as she requested of him and would not drink it but he did take a small sip so as not to pass up entirely this additional chance to suffer.

---

[178] Quote from the Mystical City of God by Mary of Agreda.

It was now very close to noon as the executioners ripped off his outer cloak. They unbuckled the leather belt to which the ropes had been tied and then took off his own belt. They tore the crown of thorns off his head with such brutal force that some of the thorns remained in his head and the blood ran freely down into his eyes, ears and mouth. They pulled his one piece tunic up and over his head leaving him clad in only his undershirt and a loin cloth. The undershirt was made of wool and had stuck itself to the wounds on his chest, back and shoulders which had been made by the carrying of the heavy cross and the scourging. They ripped off his undershirt reopening many of his wounds while tearing off pieces of hanging flesh. The pain caused by this action was inhuman and the blood flowed freely down his mangled frame. [179]

When they tried to remove his loin cloth once again they could not do so as before. It will remain on him even in the tomb.

Our Lord trembled uncontrollably. He was exhausted, cold and suffering horrible pain and a high fever. Seeing that he was about to sag and fall the executioners dragged him to a nearby rock and sat him down while they attended to some last minute details.

Putting this lull in the activities to good use Our Blessed Lord prayed to his Eternal Father saying; "Eternal Father and My Lord God, to the incomprehensible majesty of your infinite goodness and justice I offer my humanity and all that according to your will it has accomplished in descending from your bosom to assume passable and mortal flesh for the redemption of men, my brethren; I offer you Lord with myself, also my most loving Mother, her love, her most perfect works, her sorrows, her sufferings, her anxious and perfect solicitude in serving me,

---

[179] Six times during the passion they removed his clothes. First in the cell beneath the house of Ciaphas to mock him. Second in Herod's palace to dress him as a fool. Third in Pilate's courtyard to scourge him. Fourth in the Antonio courtyard to dress him in a cape and mock his as a king. Fifth at Gabbatha to dress him in his own garments and sixth on Calvary to shame and crucify him. A multitude of sins are committed without clothing on. In order to atone for them he is reduced many times to nakedness which is so abhorrent and humiliating to his most pure nature.

imitating me and accompanying me unto death. I offer you the little flock of my Apostles, the Holy Church and congregation of the faithful such as it is now and as it shall be until the end of the world and with it I offer you all the mortal children of Adam. All this I place in your hands as the true and Almighty Lord and God. As far as my wishes are concerned I suffer and die for all and I desire that all be saved under condition that all follow me and profit of my redemption. Thus may they pass from the slavery of the devil to be your children, my brethren and co-heirs of the grace merited by me. Especially Oh Lord do I offer you the poor, the despised and the afflicted who are my friends and who follow me on the way to the cross. I desire that the just and the predestined be written on your Eternal Memory. I beseech you my Father to withhold your chastisement and not raise the scourge of your justice over men. Let them not be punished as they merit for their sins. Be, from now on, their Father as you are mine. I beseech you also that they may be helped to ponder upon my death in pious affection and be enlightened from above and I pray for those who are persecuting me in order that they may be converted to the truth. Above all, I do ask you for the exaltation of your ineffable and Most Holy Name." [180]

The Holy Mother was not only aware of her Son's prayer but offered all the same petitions in union with him humbly accepting all the grief, pain and suffering it would bring upon both of them. When the prayer was finished the Blessed Virgin came up to her Son and taking his hands into hers kissed them and adored him in a most reverent manner. No one objected as his enemies though that the nearness of his Mother would cause him even greater pain and anguish of heart. They had no clue as to how much she consoled him.

When the executioners came for him the Blessed Mother stepped aside without being asked to. They grabbed him off the rock and half walked and half dragged him to the cross. He unsteadily stood before his wooden torture rack a mass of bleeding wounds. Pieces of raw flesh hung everywhere from his mangled and tortured body. White bloodstained bones were

---

[180] Quote from the Mystical City of God by Mary of Agreda.

155

sickeningly visible in many places on his shoulders and rib cages front and rear. His face was a grotesque distortion of its former self and horrible to look upon. His hands and feet were so puffed and swollen as to have a bloated appearance.. His hair and beard were matted with fresh flowing blood and gobs of clotted blood in those areas where it had not yet been pulled out. His overall condition was beyond belief, traumatized beyond natural life, tormented beyond words and still very much alive and he was suffering horribly.

The Son of God, the Messiah, the most innocent of all the innocent, the purest of the pure and the holy of holies stood naked on Calvary, so crushed by the weight of our sins that as St Paul says; "He is become sin! He is made a curse for our sake." The heavy burden of the wrath of God for all these sins is upon him. He is the lone representatives of a lost race of blind humanity in dire need of redemption and the remedy lay before him at his feet. The cross!

They ordered him to lie down on the cross so they could nail him to it. He did so with out hesitation and stretched out his hands voluntarily to receive the nails. The executioners grabbed his right hand and placed it over the hole they had drilled in the wood to receive the large blunt nail. [181] They tied his arm tightly to the cross. One of the executioners kneeled on his chest while another held down his hand. A third drove the nail into the thick part of the hand just above the bend line of the wrist. [182] When the nail was firmly in place they turned their attention to his left hand. They had purposely drilled the holes in the wood too far apart as they had intended from the beginning to stretch him out on the cross to increase his sufferings. They looped a chain around his left hand and pulled violently until the hand was over the hole, dislocating his bones and ripping and tearing muscles, tendons, blood vessels and nerves in the process. No words can

---

[181] There is a tradition that it was the sixth day of the week (Friday) at the sixth hour (noon) that Adam stretched out his right hand to sin against God.

[182] Due to the poor quality of the nails of that time period it is very likely that holes were drilled into the hands and feet before nailing to damage the tissue enough to allow the nails to be driven in. A form of hand drill called a gimlet would have been used.

describe the pain. His chest heaved outward as his spine curved up and pulled his legs up into a fetal position. They tied his hand to the cross and again one of them kneeled on his chest while another held his hand down and a third drove the nail home.

When making the preparations for the cross they had nailed a block of wood to the upright beam to act as a foot support. Doing so allowed the condemned to push up on his feet to take in air when breathing became difficult, prolonging death and increasing suffering. Because of the violent stretching Our Lord's body had been severely contorted and pulled upward and his legs were bent and twisted.

They flattened out his body and legs and tied them tightly to the beam and started to curse and swear when they saw that his feet did not reach the block. Now they had to decide between two choices; take the nails out of the hands and start over or attempt to stretch him out until he reached the foot block. After a short discussion they looped the chain around his feet and pulled them down to the block dislocating the legs and hips again ripping sinews, muscles, blood vessels, nerves and tendons causing excruciating pain. Even after all this inhumanity they were not finished with him yet. They nailed his right foot to the left side of the blocks surface then crossed his left foot over the right and nailed it to the right side of the blocks surface, not only to increase the pain but to make it even more difficult to push up on the feet and take in more air when necessary. [183]

The agony Our Lord is undergoing at this point defies description. Every inch of his mangled body is stretched, ripped and distended. All his bones are wracked and dislocated with every muscle in spasm which severely contorts his body into

---

[183] To make it clear in your mind how the feet were nailed, stand up and hold on to something so you won't fall. Now cross your left foot over your right, hold them flat on the floor at even length and as close together as possible. This is how he was nailed. The common belief is that three nails were used. The facts don't agree. When the true cross was discovered there were four nails with it of equal length. None were long enough to penetrate two feet at once. The Church still maintains these precious relics in its possession. The poor quality of the nails in that time period would make it unlikely that a nail of the required length would have worked.

grotesque shapes. All the wounds inflicted on him earlier in the day are stretched open and the blood is flowing freely again. He is tied and nailed to the cross so tightly that he could not move if he wanted to. He is gasping more than breathing and the ever present pain is beyond excruciating and it will only get worse with the passage of each minute. The pain is so severe that even being slow roasted to death would be of no comparison and at this point, only death can free him from it.

Through it all his Holy Mother is being tormented in her own body in complete conformity with her Son's sufferings although only he is aware of what she is going through. Those around her are not aware of her sufferings which are so severe that without aid from above she would have most certainly died.

The executioners now decide to turn the cross over so that they can bend the nails back that have penetrated the wood so they won't pull out when they raise the cross up and his weight begins to pull at them. As they begin to lift the cross to flip it over, the Blessed Virgin commands the Angels of her guard to go to the assistance of their creator and not to allow them to dump him face downward on the rock surface of the mount. They caught the cross as it approached the ground but held it so closely above it that it appeared to everyone present that he had hit the ground. Some gasps went up from some of those standing around and for the first time some sympathetic comments were heard.

When the executioners had finished their brutal work the Roman commander Quintus Cornelius [184] approached and ordered them to fasten Pilate's banner to the top of the cross. The Pharisees immediately began to argue with the Centurion against placing the banner on the cross at all. He informed them that Pilate's orders would be carried out. They especially became angry when some of the Roman soldiers began chiding them and pointing out their king to them. Seeing that they were getting

---

[184] It is unknown if this is the same Centurion Cornelius who will later on send a message to Joppa for St Peter to come to Caesarea at the inspiration of the Holy spirit and be baptized with all his family. The connection could not be made but one can only wonder how many Centurions were surnamed Cornelius in this particular Legion.

nowhere with their arguments they rushed off in a huff to the Praetorium to attempt to get Pilate to order a change in the inscription.

When the banner was in place, they returned the crown of thorns to his head to remain there once and for all until the hour of his death.

The executioners dragged the cross to the hole in which they planned to erect it with Our Lord still face down. Tying ropes to the cross some of them pulled it from the back while others lifted and pushed upwards from the front. Many put their shoulders into it while some of the soldiers pushed on parts of the cross with their spears and halberds. [185] Some of them even jammed the spears into his armpits so they wouldn't slip, wounding Our Lord severely as they pushed up. Suddenly the cross dropped into the hole with a violent thud causing crushing pain to all his distended parts and opening some of his many wounds even more, especially the nail wounds. With the cross upright, some of them held it steady while others hammered in wedges around its base to hold it fast.

With the cross firmly secured they put the ladders up against it and unfastened the ropes with which they had tied his arms, body and legs so that his body would only be fastened by the nails. This allowed his distended body to sag on his dislocated limbs increasing the pain tenfold. Now to breathe fully or to talk he will have to pull and push himself up on his contorted limbs causing himself even greater pain.

The ropes had been so tight that they had interfered with his blood circulation. With the ropes off the blood came rushing back into his limbs causing great discomfort.

Hanging freely on the nails his pain increases with each second. His body droops and sags and for a time he hangs motionless as if dead but in reality he is offering a lengthy prayer to his Eternal Father.

He prayed: "I praise you Father as the Eternal God and I confess and magnify you from the tree of this cross. I offer you a

---

[185] A halberd is a type of spear which also has an axe head just below the spear point. Two weapons in one.

sacrifice of praise in my passion and death for by the hypostatic union with the Divine Nature you have raised my humanity to the highest dignity, that of Christ the God-Man, anointed with your own divinity. You have consigned to me full dominion of the universe in the order of grace and nature. You have made me Lord of the heavens and the elements, of the sun, the moon and stars; of fire and air, of earth and sea and of all the animate and inanimate creatures therein. You have set me as the head, the King and Lord of all Angels and Men to govern and command them, to punish the wicked and to reward the good. You have given me the dominion and the power of disposing all things from the highest Heavens to the deepest abyss of hell. You have placed in my hands the eternal justification of men and all that are capable of grace and glory. You have made me the justifier, redeemer and glorifier, the universal Lord of all the human race, of life and death, of the Holy Church; its treasures, laws and blessings of grace.

Now, my Lord and Father I am returning to your right hand from this world through my death on the cross by which I complete the task assigned to me. I have sought to gain all mortals and invited them to partake of my friendship and grace. From the moment of my incarnation I have ceaselessly labored for them. I have born inconveniences, fatigues, ignominies, insults, reproaches, scourges, a crown of thorns and now I suffer the bitter death of the cross. In our knowledge and foresight we are aware, my God and Father, that on account of their rebellious obstinacy not all men desire to accept our eternal salvation nor avail themselves of our mercy but prefer to follow their sinful way into perdition.

I desire that all who dispose themselves shall partake of the goods of my Holy Church and of the Sacraments; that if they should lose my friendship they shall be able to restore themselves and recover my graces and blessings through my cleansing blood. For to all of them shall be open the intercession of my Mother and of all the Saints and she shall recognize them as her own. My Angels shall defend them, guide them and bear them up and if they fall help them to rise again.

I wish to hold with them my delights, communicate to them my secrets, converse with them intimately and live with them in the Militant Church in the species of bread and wine.

As for those who have done all in opposition to our Divine goodness and remain obstinate in their malice and since they have renounced the rights of son ship merited for them by me, I disinherit them of my friendship and glory, separating them from our company and from that of my Mother and of the Angels and saints. I condemn them to the eternal dungeons and the fire of hell in the company of Lucifer and his demons whom they have freely served. I deprive them forever of all hope of relief.

This Oh Father is the sentence I pronounce as the head and judge of men and Angels and this is the testament made at my death. This is the effect of my redemption whereby each one is rewarded with that which he has justly merited according to his works and your wisdom and justice. [186]

In the Hinnom Valley, Judas stood at the edge of the Brook Kidron at a point southwest of the city wall. He was incensed at how badly things had turned out for him. .

Satan continued to torment his thoughts reminding him that it was at this very spot where David crossed over the Kidron running from his rebellious son Absalom and that Absalom had hanged himself. [187]

Satan said to Judas; " It was of you that David spoke when he said: "They have repaid me evil for good! Hatred for my love! May the devil stand at his right hand when he is judged and may he go out condemned! May his days be few and his Bishopric let another take. May the iniquity of his father be remembered in the sight of the Lord and let not the sin of his mother be blotted out because he remembered not to show mercy but persecuted the poor man, the beggar and the broken heart to put him to death. He loved cursing and it shall come back to him

---

[186] This is a synopsis of a much longer prayer which is quoted in the Mystical City of god by Mary of Agreda, pages 666 to 672 inclusive in the third volume.

[187] This was not true. Absalom had ridden his mount under a tree in which his long flowing hair had become entangled in the branches and he was found hanging their helpless by one of David's men, who killed him.

and he put on cursing like a garment and it went in like water to his belly and like oil to his bones. May it be to him like a garment which covers him like a girdle with which he is girdled continually. [188]

Satan has no more use for Judas and is trying to tempt him to despair of his life and to kill himself.

Judas gave in to the temptation to despair, made his way across the Kidron to a wild portion of Mount Olivet far south of the Garden of Gethsemane to an area which was largely used for a garbage dump. He rejected all grace. He rejected the notion that his Master was the Messiah and the Son of God and therefore rejected the Eucharist. Lastly, he rejected his apostolic commission and was despondent that he had failed in his quest to gain power and wealth.

Feeling that he had nothing more to live for he gave in to despair and using his own belt hung himself from a tree which jutted out from a cleft in the rocks. His neck broke with such horrible force that his belly ruptured and his insides spilled out onto the ground below him. This occurred at about the same time that his Former Master was being crucified. Demons came at once and took his soul down to hell.

While Our Lord was being crucified, the two thieves had been made to recline on the ground at the foot of Calvary still tied to their crossbeams. They had been part of a band of thugs and robbers that operated mostly along the Egyptian frontier and had been convicted of murder and robbery and sentenced to die by crucifixion.

Now that Our Lord was nailed and hung up the executioners turned their attention to them. They brought them to the summit, gave them the drink of vinegar and myrrh and took off all their clothing. As their upright beams were already securely fastened in the ground they tied ropes to their cross

---

[188] Satan is quoting Psalm 108. Notice how he is willing to even quote scripture to gain his ends. This is a good example of how we can be expected to be accosted at the hour of our own death. That is why we must be prepared and seek the protection of the Church and its Sacraments along with the intercession of the Blessed Virgin and the Angels and Saints.

beams and dragged them up into place. They crucified one to Our Lord's right and one to his left. [189] There is enough room between the crosses for the Centurion to ride his horse through. Our Lord's cross had been purposely placed in the middle to show everyone that he is the worst of the lot. For his part, Our Lord is dying for sinners and so he chooses to die with sinners. Our Lord looks upon his two companions with the greatest compassion and in union with his Holy Mother he prays fervently for their conversion. Gesmas cursed and swore at length while Dismas hung quietly.

The executioners divided Our Lord's clothes into four separate piles but didn't rip his one piece tunic as they didn't wish to ruin it. They decided among themselves it was better to gamble for his clothes, which they did. [190] When they had finished gambling and decided who was to get what, they were approached by a servant of Nicodemus and Joseph of Arimathea with an offer to by the garments. It was an offer too good to refuse so they took the money and surrendered the blood stained garments to the servant.

Their work being done, the executioners gathered up their equipment and left Calvary.

At about this time a new unit of Roman soldiers, about fifty in number marched up to Calvary to relieve the troops who had overseen the procession and crucifixion. [191] The Centurion who is to take command of the hill is called Abenadar and the Centurion Cassius Gaius is his second in command. By order of Pilate, the two hundred troops now on Calvary which are commanded by the Centurion Quintus Cornelius will be

---

[189] Dismas to the right and Gesmas to the left. During the flight to Egypt many years before the mother of Dismas had given shelter to the Holy family.
Dismas had been cured of leprosy as a child after being dipped in bathwater that had been use to bathe the holy child.

[190] It was the accepted custom of the times that the executioners were entitled to the belongings of the condemned.

[191] This is a good military move by Pilate. With the troops which oversaw the crucifixion now leaving and as the relief troops had nothing to do with any of it, tension would be somewhat relieved.

redeployed to the gates around the walled city to guard against any possibility of civil unrest.

The Pharisees, Scribes and Sadducees who had left the hill in a huff to go to the Praetorium to get Pilate to change the wording on the banner had returned with the new troops. They were in a foul mood as they had received a flat refusal form the Governor to their request. They threw stones and dirt at Our Lord's cross and said; "You that destroy the Temple of God and in three days build it up again, save yourself; come down from the cross and we will believe." Some of the soldiers chimed in and echoed the sentiments of the Jewish leaders also telling Our Lord to come down from the cross. One soldier stepped forward, took a sponge, filled it with vinegar, stuck it on a spear and lifted it up to Our Lord saying at the same time; "If you are the king of the Jews, save yourself and come down from the cross." [192]

While all this is going on Our Lord struggles to pull himself up on his tortured arms and to push up on his contorted legs. He gasps all the air he can into his burning lungs and says; "Father forgive them; for they know not what they do." [193] For a moment everyone is stunned by what they hear and stare in silence at the figure on the middle cross. They had never heard nor had they ever expected to hear such words from a dying crucified. No one made any response.

Quintus Cornelius formed up his troops and marched them off the mount to redeploy them at the various city gates in

---

[192] Notice the change in rhetoric. A short time ago it was; "Crucify him! Crucify him! Now it's; "Come down from the cross! Satan is feeling a terrible power being exercised over him by the cross. He wants to flee Calvary but is not allowed to; so he incites the cry to come down.

[193] He not only sincerely forgives all his tormentors but points out the fact that they may not be completely aware of what they are doing. The soldiers and executioners are carrying out a routine execution although no one forced them to be as brutal as they were. The Priests and leaders of the people know exactly what they are doing but it is not probable that they completely understood the magnitude of their crime. He is not excusing them but just recognizing the facts. St Augustine says; "That by this most merciful prayer he was hindering their damnation. He is also showing that he hates the sin but loves the sinner.

compliance with the Governor's orders, leaving the hill and the crucifixion site to the command of Abenadar.

The trumpets which had been sounding in the Temple precincts stopped blowing, signifying that it was time for the sacrifice of the Paschal lambs.

The Holy Mother Mary, seeing all that was going on; how men dishonored and defiled her Divine Son as the most wicked among men fell down flat to the ground at the foot of the cross and adored him as only she was capable. She requested God the Father to honor his only Begotten Son by causing evident signs to appear in nature that would confuse men and frustrate their dishonorable intentions. The Eternal Father granted the request of his beloved daughter and gave her the right and power to command nature.

She promptly addressed all creation and said; "Insensible creatures, created by the hand of the Almighty, do you manifest your compassion which in deadly foolishness is denied to him by men capable of reason. You heavens, you sun, you moon, you stars and planets stop in your course and suspend your activity. You elements change your condition, earth loose your stability; let your rocks and cliffs be rent. You sepulchers and monuments of the dead open up and send forth your contents for the confusion of the living. You mystical and figurative veil of the Temple divide into two parts and by your separation threaten the unbelievers with chastisement. Give witness to the truth and to the glory of their creator and redeemer which they are trying to obscure. [194]

Rapidly, the sun began to lose its light even though it was high in the sky and fully visible. As the darkness settled in, the stars and moon became visible and due to the ever increasing red mist appeared blood red. A large foreboding shadow filled the sky and overpowered the sun. An eerie yellow glow dominated its center and it was surrounded by a red fiery ring. It was now as dark as night. [195] Birds began falling out of the sky unable to fly

---

[194] Quote from the Mystical City of God by Mary of Agreda.
[195] About the year two hundred, Tertullian, one of the early Church Fathers was speaking to the Romans about this very occurrence during the crucifixion

because of the rapid onset of this sudden darkness. They emitted frightening squawks and shrieks. Throughout the city and neighboring countryside the mournful bleating and lowing of terrified animals were enough to send chills up and down anyone's spine. The stars emitted a fiery red light and the moon moved back and forth across the sky like a red fireball. [196]

At first, the Pharisees tried to explain what was happening using their limited reason but soon fell silent as the events progressed. Soldiers, Pharisees, bystanders and beasts were all terrified together. All became silent. Some struck their breasts and fell to their knees begging forgiveness as the darkness and frightening events in the sky increased. [197]

Seeing these events Gesmas cried out; "If you are the Christ, save yourself and us." Our Lord did not answer him.

Dismas had been deeply moved by the prayer of Our Lord forgiving all his enemies, now, witnessing all the strange events that are taking place all around him he is seized with fear. [198] Grace from the prayers of Our Lord and his Holy Mother is beginning to bear fruit in the soul of Dismas. Enlightened by this grace he remembers his childhood cure of leprosy and realizes that these are the people responsible. Responding to the grace at work in him he rebukes Gesmas saying; "Do you not fear God seeing that you are under the same condemnation and we indeed justly, for we receive the due reward for our deeds but this man had done no evil."

Then he poured out his heart and soul to his Lord and God and confessed all his sins. Then turning to Our Lord in all humility and with a completely contrite heart he said; "Lord, remember me when you come into your Kingdom." The Savior

---

and told them; "You yourselves have recorded this great event in your annals." The event had been documented in official Roman records.

[196] Much like the miracle of the sun, centuries later at Fatima in Portugal.

[197] The prophet Joel spoke of this darkness in his prophecy;"The sun shall be turned into darkness and the moon into blood." The Prophet Amos said; "For the day of the Lord, the sun would go down at noon." The Gospels do not mention the moon turning red, but many of the early Church Fathers say that it happened.

[198] Fear of the Lord is the beginning of wisdom!

166

replied; "Amen, I say to you, this day you shall be with me in Paradise,"[199]

Mary and her companions were standing a short distance from the cross when they heard Our Lord promise Paradise to Dismas and the tender heart of the loving Mother was overwhelmed with love and gratitude at the acceptance of grace and the humble conversion of Dismas. At the same time, however, she was also aware of the demise of Judas and his refusal to accept the graces offered to him. The loss of the wayward Apostle was an occasion if immense grief to her but it did not lessen the joy of the conversion of Dismas for each one had made his own free choice.

Even still, in her heart, mind, spirit and body she was suffering intensely all that her Divine Son was suffering. Her body was on fire with pain and it was just as difficult for her to move about as it was for him to push himself up to speak; but move she did to the very foot of the cross and her companions followed. Looking up at her Divine Son she requested permission from him to be allowed to die with him. He looked upon her with and expression of deepest love for he knew all too well what she was suffering and offering.

With great difficulty he said to her; Woman, behold your son." Then speaking to John he said; "Behold your Mother." [200] She knows immediately in her heart of hearts that he is saying farewell and that when he finally yields to death that she must remain. What a sword of sorrow pierces her soul.

Over the entire expanse of Calvary and its vicinity no one can be heard speaking. Not the crucified, not the soldiers, no

---

[199] In the depths of his abandonment, Our Lord has found a friend. The fruits of the redemption are already at work. Dismas professed his guilt for all to hear and at the same time manifested the innocence of his Lord also for all to hear. His words are a strong condemnation of all those who have sought the death of Our Lord for if he has done no evil, then great must be the evil of those who wanted him dead.

[200] He calls her Woman and not Mother. God had promised in the Garden of Eden that he would put enmity between Satan and the Woman and her seed would crush his head. He is confessing to the entire world that she is the woman and he as her Son is fulfilling the prophecy.

bystanders, not even his enemies. All have been reduced to silence by the midday darkness and the events taking place in the sky. Occasionally the deathly silence is broken by the ghastly screeching of the birds or the pathetic cry of the jittery animals which only shatters everyone's nerves. No one attempts to move about in the darkness as no one came prepared for darkness. To add to all the other fears, the earth is now trembling at a constant rate, rattling doors and windows throughout the city and causing a constant sensation of movement beneath everyone's feet. [201] Many sink to the ground and pull their veils over their heads as if to protect themselves from some impending disaster. At times, soft crying and lamentations pierce the silence.

When these strange events began to occur, Herod hurried to the Praetorium to confer with Pilate. They stood on the terrace overlooking the paved courtyard and discussed the events as they watched them unfold. They agreed that what they were observing was definitely outside the normal course of nature and that the gods must be upset with the treatment of the Nazarene.

Under heavy guard, the two leaders went on foot to the palace of Herod and then summoned some of the council members and demanded to know their explanation of the events now taking place. Herod and Pilate advised the councilors that they were in agreement that the God of the Jews was extremely displeased at the treatment of the Nazarene who must assuredly be what they denied him to be; namely a Prophet and a King. Pilate also reminded them that none of this had anything to do with him as he had washed his hands of the whole affair.

The obstinate council members informed Pilate and Herod that nothing was going on that intelligent men could not explain although they offered no explanation and that they were not apologetic for any of the actions the council had taken. Pilate and Herod dismissed the council members and agreed that all they had told them was nothing but utter nonsense.

Pilate returned with his guard to the Praetorium. A short time later a mob began to form in the paved courtyard. From

---

[201] The Prophet Amos had prophesied that on the day of the Lord the land would tremble. (Chap: 8 Vs 8-9).

inside the Praetorium Pilate could hear the shouts of: "down with the iniquitous judge! May the blood of the just man fall upon his murderers!" [202] This made Pilate uneasy and he sent to the Fortress Antonio for more troops. When they were in place he went out to the mob and put all the blame squarely on the Jews. He again referred to his own innocence and reminded them that he was no follower of the Galilean whom they were putting to death. He informed the crowd that he was their Prophet, their King and their Holy Man not his and he reminded them that as far as he was concerned they alone were guilty of this mans death as they had forced him to condemn the Galilean. [203]

The Temple area was packed with people who had come for the sacrifice of the Paschal lamb but when the darkness had begun to rapidly descend and reached the point where it was difficult to see and the sun, moon and stars began to act in a manner never witnessed before, the crowd began to panic and remorseful cries and petitions began to arise throughout the structure. All the lanterns were ordered lit and the Priests tried to maintain order but eventually all ceremonies came to a halt. Annas was almost out of his mind with fear and frantically ran back and forth looking for a place to hide himself.

On Calvary, the Blessed Savior hung in miserable agony. The darkness which covered all the land was only a hint of the darkness that tormented his soul. A horrid bitterness penetrated his entire being and in the midst of his most bitter agony he prayed to his Eternal Father for his enemies. He desired their conversion, not their loss. He was at this very moment deprived of all consolation and kept praying the Psalms which contained the prophecies which he was now bringing to fulfillment. In his humanity he grieved as he had done in he Garden over the loss of souls and once again desired the salvation of all in light of the immense merits of his passion. Moved to the deepest sorrow over

---

[202] Quote from the Dolorous Passion of Our Lord Jesus Christ by Anne Catherine Emmerich.

[203] Two things catch the eye here. Pilate, a pagan is expressing his belief that Our Lord is a Prophet, a King and a Holy man just as he had done to the council members at Herod's Palace. At the same time he exonerates himself from any wrong doing in Our Lord's death.

the loss of so many who would reject him and his offers of salvation he pushed up on the nails in his feet and painfully pulled up on his wounded hands, gasped for breath to fill his lungs and broke the eerie silence by saying loudly; "My God! My God! Why have you forsaken me?" [204]

The Pharisees turned toward him and said; "Look he calls Elias. Let us see whether Elias will come to deliver him"

Shortly after this he raised himself up again and said;" I Thirst." A soldier soaked a sponge in wine vinegar and placing it on a reed of hyssop raised it to his lips but he turned his head away and did not drink, [205]

It was now drawing close to the ninth hour (Three PM). The moon by now had settled into its normal place and the light of day was slowly beginning to return. Our Divine lord was at the dregs of his sufferings. He has given all there is to give. He is so drained mentally that he is on the verge of insanity. Morally he is at the point of a soul about to enter hell. His physical pain has steadily increased throughout the three hours to a point beyond death where the addition of pain is not possible. He has given so completely of himself for the redemption of mankind that there is simply nothing more to give. He is in he final throes of death when he utters; "It is consummated!" [206]

He raised his eyes to Heaven and in a loud voice for all to hear said; "Father into your hands I commend my spirit!" He bowed his head and gave up his life.

While the Holy Mother did not die with him she still suffered all the pains and sorrows of his most bitter death. [207]

---

[204] These are the opening lines of Psalm twenty one which Our Lord is undoubtedly reciting but also in his humanity he still desires that all be saved but in his Divinity he knows that he cannot impose himself upon those who freely reject him. Therefore he suffers the bitterness of abandonment.

[205] His thirst was for souls, not liquids. He desired that all should benefit from his merits and sufferings. His thirst was a deep expression of his love for humanity. This is the reason he is willing to endure all these biter sufferings.

[206] All that he had come into the world to do is now accomplished. It is now time to leave it.

[207] Is it any wonder the Church bestows on her the title co-redemptrix. .

Chapter VII
The Aftermath

His Holy Mother understood that when her Divine Son said; "It is consummated," that not only his earthly life was over but the hour of the power of darkness was also at an end. Never again would his enemies have any power to do him any harm. Lifting her eyes to Heaven she asked the Eternal Father to glorify his Son and at the same time requested that all his works bless the Lord also.

It is now three O'clock in the afternoon, the time for the evening sacrifice in the Temple on Mount Moriah. The trumpets can be heard throughout the city and on Calvary as well calling the people to the evening sacrifice. Little do they understand that the evening sacrifice has just concluded with Our Lord's death and that the only acceptable sacrifice is already slain. What they are preparing to do in the Temple has just faded into history and is no longer pleasing or acceptable to God.

The only response to the Temple trumpets is the response to the Blessed Virgins prayer that her Son be glorified and blessed by the elements. A faint rumbling begins deep within the earth as the ground begins to tremble beneath their feet. The horse of Abenadar shakes beneath him as it fights to keep its footing. Many fall to the ground as the tremors rapidly become more violent. Suddenly the rock is rent in two as Calvary moves beneath their feet with a tremendous roar and a great split opens up between the cross of Our Lord and the cross of Gesmas to his left. At the same instance a portion of the west wall behind Calvary crumbles and many buildings begin to fall throughout the city.

In the great Temple, the two pillars which stood before the holy of holies and supported the great veil which covered it began to move and then fell away from each other ripping the veil in two from top to bottom [208] exposing the inner sanctuary. A voice was heard to say; "Let us leave this place."

The soul of Our Blessed Lord entered into Paradise the moment he died. His first action was to direct a large number of souls to reenter the same bodies in which they had lived while on earth and to give testimony before the living of his Divinity. [209]

On Calvary most people were terrified beyond description. Many ripped their garments and threw dust over their heads as a sign of repentance. The last loud cry of Our Lord had filled them with dread and all of them equated the earthquake to his death. They trembled and moaned expecting worse to follow. Many struck their breasts and asked for forgiveness. Even the soldiers were tense and apprehensive bracing themselves for whatever might happen next.

Gradually the rumbling stopped and the earth stood still. The air had become thick and oppressive making it difficult to breathe. Not a sound was heard from anyone as all eyes were on the cross waiting to see if these terrible events were at an end or if more tremors were to come.

Abenadar sat on his horse gazing up at the figure on the cross. His eyes had witnessed many strange and unexplainable events this day. Strange omens in the sky, darkness in the middle of the day, words of forgiveness by a man who had been wronged at every level and by every one; and now this earthquake. Suddenly taking up his lance, which is the symbol of his authority he threw it as far away from himself as he could and then in a voice loud enough for all in the vicinity to hear said; "Blessed be the Most High God, the God of Abraham, of Isaac and Jacob; indeed this man was the Son of God."

The bystanders and Pharisee's were stunned. His fellow soldiers looked at him in wide eyed wonder. They too had

---

[208] The ripping in two from top to bottom in Jewish customs always signified blasphemy. Recall how Ciaphas had ripped his garments in tow from top to bottom during the religious trial. The killing of Our Lord was the ultimate blasphemy.

[209] St Jerome takes it for granted that these souls rose from the dead in the same way as Lazarus, only to have to die again after they had given witness. St Thomas Aquinas agrees.

witnessed all the abnormal events for which there seemed no explanation. Now their Centurion, a man whom they trusted and whose wisdom and good judgment they relied on was confessing this man on the middle cross to be the Son of the Most High God. Was not this the same man that only a few short hours ago had been crowned and mocked in the Antonio courtyard which they themselves had witnessed? Could this possibly be? Some of them came to believe along with their Centurion but not all.

The Blessed Mother turned and looked intently at Abenadar. How she had prayed through all the passion for the conversion of all mankind even amid all her horrible sufferings and here again the fruit of her intercessory labors was beginning to show. What joy filled her tender and loving Mother's heart at the conversion of the Roman Officer. [210]

Abenadar sent one of his soldiers to retrieve his lance. When the soldier returned with the lance, He dismounted from his horse and handed the reins to the Centurion Cassius Gaius. Then taking the lance from the soldier he gave it to Cassius, thereby transferring his authority of command and placing him in charge of the detail.

He then left Calvary on foot by himself and went down through the Valley of Gihon into the Hinnom Valley in search of the Apostles so that he could give them an account of all that had taken place. [211] After he found the Apostles and related his story to them he started back across the city to report to Pilate.

The earthquake had done a great deal of damage throughout all of Israel but had taken its greatest toll in

---

[210] (Luke Chap: 10) "You have hidden these truths from the wise and have revealed them to the little ones." (Mark Chap: 10) "Many that are first shall be last and the last first." St Bernard writes; "sure sighted faith recognized God in the crib (magi), on the cross (thief), in death (Centurion)."

[211] It seems ironic that when the Temple guards converted they knew in what direction to head to find the Apostles and now this Centurion. There is a belief that Abenadar, who was an Arab by birth, had converted to Judaism earlier and had heard Christ speak. It is also possible that he may have been the Centurion whose servant boy was cured at Caesarea but there is no confirmation of that.

Jerusalem. [212] It came at about the same time that daylight was beginning to return and most peoples fears were beginning to subside. Then the earthquake suddenly hit amidst a great deal of noise and sparked immense confusion as buildings began to crack and crumble. When the rumbling finally stopped and before they had a chance to recover their wits and collect themselves they were suddenly confronted by people whom they knew were dead, still clad in their burial wrappings with only their faces showing.

These dead people made their way about in pairs loudly professing the innocence of Our Lord and proclaiming to all his Divinity. They approached in an accusatory manner and read the citizens of Jerusalem the riot act; severely reprimanding them for the part they had played in the death of this innocent man. The people of Jerusalem were thrown into an absolute state of panic and horror by the appearance of these moving talking cadavers.

In the Temple itself, the festivities had been halted because of the absolute darkness but had been resumed by the order of the High Priests as soon as the daylight had begun to return. Just as they restarted the ceremonies the earthquake hit, disrupting them again. The Priests looked on in horror as the columns fell, ripping the veil in two and exposing the Holy of Holies. Other columns fell throughout the Temple grounds as well inducing great panic among the large crowds in and about the great Temple.

As the dust began to settle, the Priests, who always tried to maintain the strictest obedience to the law and rituals in the performance of Temple ceremonies, tried their best to calm the crowds and continue the ceremonies.

Suddenly the dead appeared in and among the crowds stunning the people and filling them with absolute terror. Just as other risen souls were doing throughout the city they began reproving the crowd in the same severe manner chastising them

---

[212] St John Chrysostom along with many early Church Fathers believed the quake was felt throughout the world. Early historical writers mention local quakes that bear out their opinion.

for causing the death of the innocent and just man and for calling his blood down upon themselves.

The former High Priest Zachariah, who had been murdered in the Temple, appeared in the sanctuary and proclaimed fearful woes and spoke of the death of the second Zachariah who was murdered for not betraying his son John the Baptist. He also spoke of the death of John and all the other Prophets who had been slain.

The two deceased Sons of the former High Priest Simon appeared in the Temple area which was normally occupied by the doctors of the law. They also brought up the death of the Prophets and informed all present that the sacrifice of the old law was at an end and told them to embrace the doctrine which had been preached by the crucified one.

The Prophet Jeremiah appeared by the great Altar and also informed them that a new sacrifice had started and that the old one had now ended.

These latter appearances by former Priests and Prophets took place in the areas of the Temple which were mainly frequented by Priests and for the most part were denied or concealed from the general population. [213]

Even though the High Priests and the ruling class were scared out of their wits, their hardened diabolical hearts would not listen even to the preaching of the dead. [214]

Annas, the most insistent and persistent enemy of Our Lord; the one who pushed constantly more than any other for his demise and who was behind almost every effort to ensnare him and put him to death was almost out of his mind with fear. He ran back and forth like a chicken with his head cut off trying to find a place to hide; especially after the earthquake hit. Ciaphas had succeeded in quieting him down a little bit when the dead

---

[213] However, in days to come, many Priests would be converted.

[214] (Luke, Chap: 16, Vs 31) In the parable of Lazarus and the rich man, the rich man who had been condemned to hell asked Abraham to send Lazarus back to his yet living brothers to warn them of the torments that awaited them in the after life. Abraham replied; "If they will not listen to Moses and the Prophets, neither will they believe if one rise again from the dead." True to the words of Abraham the ruling class will not even listen to the risen dead.

appeared in many parts of the Temple with their harsh speeches and terribly accusing tones. Annas was numb and paralyzed with unabated terror.

There were about thirty Pharisees who had been witness to everything that had taken place on Calvary and after being subjected to all the unnatural occurrences of nature; were converted. They came back into the Temple area just as all the turmoil from the appearance of the dead was in progress and could not believe their eyes at all the destruction within the Temple Precincts especially when some of the reconstruction projects hadn't even been completed yet. They were completely taken aback by the appearance of the dead and the panicky scenes that were unfolding before them. None the less, they overcame their fear and approached Annas and Ciaphas and spoke to both of them in the harshest of terms professing their belief and berating them for their actions. Now the High Priests were being chastised by both the living and the dead.

Pilate was also undergoing trial by fire. The earthquake had severely rattled the Praetorium and his nerves. No more had the earthquake subsided than a dead man appeared to him in his winding clothes and severely reproached him for having passed sentence on an innocent man. Terrified, Pilate ran from room to room but was greeted in each of them by a dead man accusing him anew. In the depths of his superstitious mind he thought that these dead men now accusing him were the many gods of the Galilean taking out their revenge on him. Terrified of these accusatory scepters, he burned incense to the false gods of Rome for protection against these unwelcome guests.

For his part, King Herod had gone off to a solitary room in his palace so that no one else could see what a miserable state of fear and panic he had been reduced to. He remained there quite alone for a very long period of time.

About one hundred dead people, clad only in the burial windings and showing only their faces were moving about at will in the city of Jerusalem, going in and out of buildings scolding and reproaching in the harshest manner while still proclaiming Our Lord's innocence and Divinity as they went. They remained out of their graves and in the area for the better part of an hour.

As the hour came to a close, they all converged on the area of Gabbatha, where Our Lord had been unjustly condemned by Pilate. They remained for a moment as if in silent contemplation; then exclaimed loudly in unison, "Glory be to Jesus forever and destruction to his enemies." [215] Then they fanned out across Jerusalem and returned to their graves.

No sooner had all the commotion settled down before the Jewish leaders pulled themselves together and sent a delegation to Pilate to request that the legs of the criminals be broken so as to hasten their deaths. The reason they gave was that they didn't want the malefactors on their crosses during the Sabbath and festival. While their was a ring of truth to this story the real reason was to get the entire affair behind them as quickly as possible as they were afraid that the people might blame them for all that had taken place and rise up in revolt.

Pilate was open to their request and was also very anxious to get these days events behind him. He issued an order for the executioners to return to Calvary and carry out their request at once.

No sooner had Pilate taken care of this problem when he was informed that a prominent Jew named Joseph of Arimathea, a very wealthy man and leading member of the Sanhedrin wished to see him. At the same time he was informed that the Centurion Abenadar had returned from Calvary with his report.

Pilate had Joseph brought in first and was greatly surprised at his request for the body of a condemned criminal. Even though he believed Joseph to be and honest and honorable man, he found it hard to believe that Our Lord was already dead.

He sent for Abenadar and had him give a full account of all that had taken place. After hearing the Centurions report he wrote out an order giving Joseph full authority to take down the body of Our Lord and give it a proper burial. [216] Then he ordered

---

[215] Quote from the Dolorous Passion of Our Lord Jesus Christ by Anne Catherine Emmerich.

[216] This was far outside the Normal procedure as criminals were normally buried in unmarked graves by the executioners amid little or no fanfare.

Abenadar to accompany Joseph back to Calvary to insure that no one questioned his orders.

Joseph and Abenadar left the Praetorium and went to a private home in the city where Nicodemus was waiting to see if Pilate was going to release the body. The matron of this particular home was also in the business of selling herbs, spices and ointments which were used in accordance with Jewish burial customs. Once assured by Joseph that they could proceed with the burial, Nicodemus gave a list of items to the woman that he wished to purchase for the burial process. Both he and Joseph gave instructions to their servants to obtain ladders, ropes and all the necessary tools needed to take down Our Lord's body and then bring them to Calvary. While the spices and herbs were being gathered together, Joseph went off to purchase the necessary burial linens.

On Calvary the Blessed Virgin was becoming concerned about what was going to happen to the sacred body of her Divine Son. She spoke to the Angels of her guard and asked them for their help in seeing to it that her Son was taken down and given a proper burial. They answered her that they were eager to help but that the Divine Will would not allow their intervention as her son still had more blood to shed at the hands of men and that only the judge who condemned him could order his body removed from the cross.

A deathly silence settled in once again over Calvary. All the rabble rousers that had wanted him dead were gone. To them there was no longer any point in sticking around as his death had not produced the desired effects of conversion in their miserable souls and the show was over. Many others had been sincerely converted and just looked on in stunned silence as if not knowing what to do next. The soldiers carried out their duties and kept a respectful distance. Their commander, Cassius, rode silently back and forth among his troops.

Our Blessed Lady pondered the words of her Angels that he still had more blood to shed. What more was there to be done that he had not already done? He had already departed this earth and still there was more blood to be shed? Then she spotted the executioners approaching Calvary and her heart sank as she

178

thought of what they might do to the lifeless body of her Son. She turned to John and the holy women and said; "Alas, now shall my affliction reach its utmost and transfix my heart! Is it possible that the executioners and the Jews are not yet satisfied with having put to death my Son and Lord? Shall they now heap more injury upon his dead body? [217]

Arriving on Calvary the executioners paid little attention to who was still present but went immediately to work. The Holy party moved away a little as they placed their ladders against the cross of Our Lord. Going up, they saw that he was already dead and began discussing among themselves whether he was really dead or just faking. They finally decided that he was too cold and stiff to be faking and took their ladders down.

They put their ladders up on the cross of Gesmas and yielding heavy clubs smashed his arms on both sides of his elbows and then broke his legs above and below his knees. Through it all Gesmas screamed wildly and cursed and swore at his tormentors. Seeing that he was taking too long to die the executioners bashed the clubs against his chest until he fell silent. Then they loosened his body from the cross and let it fall to the ground like a bag of trash.

Next, they moved to the cross of Dismas who had taken in all the barbarity they had unleashed against his fellow criminal and he knew only too well what was in store for him. He offered his death in atonement for his many sins as his body trembled uncontrollably with fear and dread at what was about to happen to him. . His eyes filled with tears of remorse and true repentance as he turned them pleadingly toward his new Mother who was already looking up at him conferring on him the grace of final perseverance.

The Holy Mother flinched as the clubs came crashing against his limbs. His body sagged down and his mouth fell open in a silent scream and gasping, he died. He was now in Paradise with his Lord.

The executioners dropped his body to the ground in the same crude manner they had done with Gesmas and then dragged

---

[217] Quote from the Mystical City of God by Mary of Agreda.

both bodies to the back side of the mount as they intended to bury them between Calvary and the west wall of the city. Leaving the bodies at the edge of the mount, they turned their attention back to the body of Our Lord as some of them were still not convinced that he was really dead.

All who were still standing around on the hill were aghast at the amount of brutality that had been used in finishing off the two thieves and became apprehensive at what they might be thinking of doing to the body of the Lord.

The Centurion was sitting astride his horse a little way off from the crosses and had watched intently as they had gone about the execution of their brutal work in disposing of the two robbers. He had suffered for many years with an affliction of the eyes that caused him to squint in order to see and to nervously bat his eyelids. Although still a young man of about twenty five he was slowly going blind and his malady was incurable. Affliction or not he had seen clearly enough the excessive cruelty of the executioners in their handling of corpses without any regard for decency and something within him was not going to allow that to happen to the body of the Galilean.

Not even fully understanding his own actions, he suddenly spurred his horse forward, rode up the hill and positioned himself between the cross of Dismas and Our Lord's and grasping the lance in both hands plunged it into the right side of Our Lord's body deep enough to penetrate the heart and for the tip to exit the left side.

The Blessed Virgin was startled by this sudden blow and at the same time was staggered by it as she felt the effects of it in her own body and soul as if she had been the one struck. The pain in her body was less then the pain that pierced her soul.[218]

In spite of her deep suffering she looked up at Cassius with pity and love in her heart and said to him; "The Almighty look upon you with eyes of mercy for the pain you caused to my soul!"[219]

---

[218] Now was the prophecy of Simeon fulfilled; "And your own soul a sword shall pierce; that out of many hearts thoughts may be revealed.

[219] Quote from the Mystical City of God by Mary of Agreda.

180

Cassius looked deep into the eyes of the Holy Mother who had just lovingly and gently admonished him. She was forgiving his actions just as this man on the cross had forgiven everyone who had abused him. He felt deep remorse for what he had just done and had no understanding at all of what had driven him to do it. He was deeply touched by her words and for the present moment would probably have liked to have been anywhere else on earth than on Calvary with his lance penetrating her Son's side.

The prayer for pardon and mercy for Cassius uttered by his Mother was heard by Our Lord and granted. As he withdrew his lance he opened up the side of Christ and blood and water issued forth with Our Lord seeing to it that some of it spattered on the face of Cassius. He immediately stopped blinking and squinting. Looking around him he could see everything with great clarity. It was apparent to all around him that he had been cured and could see them plainly. Many times over he voiced the fact that he could see and was cured of his malady.

At the same time his soul had been filled with grace and he could also see clearly who the man on the cross really was. He became fully aware that he whom he had just mutilated was his Lord and Savior, the Son of God. He got down off his horse, confessed his belief just as Abenadar had done before him and fell on his knees before the cross weeping over his sins which were now abundantly clear to him. He loudly professed his belief in the Galilean as the true God and Savior of the world and repeatedly thanked God for returning his eyesight and for the immense graces he had just received.

Some of the other soldiers had been converted when they had heard Abenadar profess his belief in the Galilean, but not many. Now they had just witnessed a genuine miracle which no one could explain away as far as they were concerned. They had known Cassius for years and could fully attest to his serious incurable eye affliction. Many of them had even ribbed him about it in the past because of his incessant squinting and blinking. They had seen him strike the body with his lance and watched as he withdrew it again. They had watched the blood and water hit his face and were now filled with wonder at his cure. All the stories they had heard about this man and his cures were true. One by one they began dropping to their knees along side their Centurion and professing their own belief until most of the fifty soldiers still on the hill were on their knees praising God. Only a few were not converted. [220]

The Holy Mother now fully understood the words of the Angels of her Guard who had told her that her Son still had more blood to shed for the love of men. She contemplated the words of Holy Simeon anew that her soul would be pierced and how the hearts of many would reveal their thoughts. Indeed her soul had been pierced and now kneeling on the ground all around her were many pagan Roman soldiers revealing the thoughts of their hearts. Gentle tears of love flowed down her cheeks as she beheld these new sons of hers. The fruits of her Sons redemption were already beginning to manifest themselves in a most wonderful way and her family was growing. [221]

The blood and water from the side of Christ had splattered onto his side, the lower part of the cross and surrounding rock. Some of it had formed into a puddle in an indent in the rock near the foot of the cross. The Blessed Virgin, John and some of the holy women set about cleaning it up. When Cassius saw what they were doing he pitched in and aided them in the clean up process. Some of the blood and water which had accumulated in the puddle was scooped into small vials and kept. [222]When they had finished the cleanup the Blessed Virgin noticed another group of men approaching Calvary carrying ladders and tools and other equipment.

---

[220] At Horeb in the desert, Moses struck the rock with his staff and water came forth to nourish all the people. (Exodus Chap: 17, Vs 6). Cassius struck the rock, the cornerstone which the builders had rejected the cornerstone of the Church and blood and water came forth to refresh all the Church until the end of time.

[221] "And if I be lifted up from the earth, will draw all things to myself." (John Chap 12, Vs 32)

[222] Cassius was given one of the vials and carried it with him for the rest of his life. It was reportedly buried with him when he was martyred. He would go down in history know as Longinus which means long spear.

Turning to John she asked him what he thought these people who were now approaching might be up to, again fearing desecration of her Sons remains. John looked them over and then told her not to fear these men as they were servants of Joseph and Nicodemus who were Disciples of her Divine Son.

In Jerusalem, fear still reigned and not many families were celebrating the Pasch as the events of the day had interfered with the sacrificing of the required lambs. The streets were virtually empty of people as Joseph, Nicodemus and Abenadar approached the Garden Gate. Many soldiers were standing guard there and the gate was closed for security reasons.

Joseph showed the soldiers the order from Pilate and Abenadar confirmed it. The soldiers were more than agreeable to let them pass but advised them that since the earthquake they had been unable to open the gate even though they had tried several times. They all approached the gate together and Joseph on impulse grabbed hold of the large bolt and easily pulled it back. The large gate swung open by itself. Among the soldiers, only Abenadar was not astonished. They passed through the gate and turned toward Calvary leaving the soldiers inspecting the gate in bewilderment.

Arriving on Calvary Joseph and Nicodemus stood speechless in front of the cross in utter disbelief of the mangled condition of the body of their Lord. They dropped weeping to their knees and remained there for some time.

Abenadar advised the executioners that Pilate had turned the body of the Galilean over to the two men who had accompanied him to the hill. The executioners seeing that they had nothing more to do went off and buried the two thieves.

While Joseph and Nicodemus were paying their respects Cassius approached Abenadar and related all that had happened since he had left. Abenadar listened joyfully as his brother soldier told him of his cure and not only of his conversion but most of those standing guard with him. Abenadar was beside himself at the acceptance of grace by his brothers in arms. They would have much to discuss in the days to come.

Joseph and Nicodemus finally got to their feet and greeted the Blessed Mother and offered their sincere condolences. The most Blessed Virgin graciously accepted their heartfelt sorrow and thanked them in advance for the service they were about to give in providing her Beloved Son with a proper burial.

They went to work immediately and placed the ladders against the back side of the cross. Joseph and Nicodemus went up the ladders and tied Our Lord's body securely to the cross in several different places using pieces of linen so it wouldn't fall when they took out the nails. Then they straightened the bent over nails of the hands and hammered them outward until they were flush with the back side of the cross. Placing a large pin against the nail tips, they hammered them through the wood of the cross. The nails fell easily away from Our Lord's hands as the weight of his body had made the holes larger. While they were doing this, Abenadar removed the nails from the feet. Cassius received the nails into his own hands one at a time and when he had all four, he respectfully placed them at the feet of the Blessed Virgin.

When the nails were all out they came down, moved the ladders around to the front of the cross and went up to begin the process of taking him down. They slowly untied the retaining linens one at a time as they carefully descended each rung of the ladder, slowly and deliberately bringing the body of Our Lord down from the cross. Abenadar, who was standing on a short stool, handled the legs. As the body neared the ground, John supported the head, Magdalene the feet, the Holy Mother his middle while Abenadar, Joseph and Nicodemus still maintained control of the arms and legs.

They carried him a short distance from the cross and laid him down on a sheet which had been spread on the ground. Mary then knelt on the ground and rested her Divine Son's head against her knees. She lovingly embraced his bruised and battered body, laying her face on his with no thought to the bloody filthy mess and wept softly. Magdalene stayed at his feet weeping and smothering them with kisses.

All were touched as they watched this mournful Mother weeping as she poured her heart and soul out to the God of all creation, Her Son. No other mother has ever mourned as deeply as no other mother has ever loved so completely.

When she had finished paying her respects, she began the process of cleaning him up as best she could. While the men had been taking the body down from the cross the women had been preparing the ointments, linens, spices and sponges which would be needed for burial preparation. She removed the crown of thorns and pulled out the thorns which had broken off and were still embedded in the flesh. She washed all his wounds which were above the waist, cleaning blood and clots out of his eyes, nostrils, ears and hair. All the blood and water used in washing was squeezed into leather jars and kept.

The Roman soldiers assisted her by filling the jars with fresh water from the nearby spring of Gihon as she required it. At times, Cassius could be seen carrying the water himself.

When she had finished the washing, she filled his ears, nostrils and wounds with perfumed ointment.

The men then carried him a little further down the hill and cleaned and anointed the lower part of his body. Then placing him on a large linen they sprinkled a kind of powder all over his entire body. They placed herbs on his lap and then put ointment in all his major wounds. Placing more herbs between his legs they wound the lower part of his body in burial linens. Then they wrapped the lower part of the body with the sheet he was laying on and fastened it together.

When the lower part of his body was completely covered, John brought the women down to where he lay. Mary tucked a piece of fine lined which had been given to her by Claudia Procula underneath his head. Magdalene took out a small vial of perfumed balm and poured the contents into the wound in his side. [223] Then they folded his arms across the front of his body, placed the remaining spices on the rest of his torso and finished to wrap his body with the sheet including his face and head and fastened it tightly.

---

[223] This was the same vial of balm she had poured on his feet and to which Judas had so strongly objected. Our Lord told her to keep it for the day of his burial. (John Chap: 12, Vs 2 to 8).

Then they transferred him onto a long shroud which Joseph had bought, laying him on it so that his feet were near one end of it. They pulled the longer end over his head and placed it all the way down the top of his body to his feet so that he was completely covered by it back and front. Then they secured it.

Once again they all gathered around the body which was now ready for burial and gave silent adoration to their crucified Lord. Suddenly his full body image appeared on the shroud just as his facial image had appeared on Seraphia's veil. Completely astonished by this miracle they unfastened the shroud and lifted its top portion to look at the materials underneath but no image was to be found on the lower material; only on the shroud.

For a short time they adored the image on the shroud and then refastened it as before. They placed the body on a stretcher which had been made of leather and two long poles. Then four of the men lifted up the stretcher and placed in on their shoulders; Nicodemus and Joseph in the front and John and Abenadar in the rear. In this manner they would carry Our Lord to his tomb.

Jewish funeral processions of the time were always led by two torch bearers and this time the job fell to two of the converted Roman soldiers. The Blessed Virgin and her companions followed closely behind her Son's body

Cassius dismissed the few soldiers who had not been converted and gave them leave to return to Antonio. The rest he formed up into ranks and fell in behind the women. [224] The one who Pilate had consistently called king would be buried with a military escort from the mightiest army the earth had to offer.

A lone figure stood high on a hill across the Gihon Valley and watched as the procession moved slowly down from Calvary turned south into the valley of Gihon, processed past the Garden Gate and turned into a beautiful garden across from the western city wall. When they entered the garden they descended into a grotto which contained a brand new tomb in which no one had

---

[224] At the same time as this earthly procession was forming the Blessed Virgin requested many choirs of Angels to join her personal guard in honoring their creator and myriads of Angels responded immediately. So they great King of the Universe had two escorts, one heavenly and one earthly.

ever been buried. It was owned by Joseph of Arimathea and had probably been intended for his own burial.

They laid Our Lord in a sepulcher within the tomb, quickly paid their final respects as the Sabbath was very near at hand and left the tomb.

The men then closed and bolted the large brass doors and rolled a large heavy stone in front of then to seal them. Then they secured a gate leading to the tomb and left.

When they had departed, the Apostle James, the brother of John, who was the lone figure observing all this, went back to the other Apostles and Disciples who were still in hiding to tell them where the body of their Master had been laid.

For the next three days, the body of Judas dangled from the tree on which he had hanged himself for all passers by to see. This suicide of the turncoat Apostle was still another condemnation of the actions of the Sanhedrin and a great embarrassment to them. No matter how many times they tried they failed in each and every attempt to bring the body down and bury it.

At the end of three days, demons came forth out of the abyss and brought the body of Judas down to hell to suffer for all eternity with his immortal soul.

Chapter VIII
The summation

First of all, in summation, this book is a dismal failure in its attempt to bring to the reader the horror of that day, in as far as understanding the sufferings which Our Lord endured, spiritually, mentally and physically. It is beyond our understanding. The main reason we cannot understand the horrible suffering of the passion is because we do not fully understand the seriousness of sin. Therefore we cannot fully appreciate the measures it took to expiate it.

Second, this book fails to impress properly upon the reader how much God loves us. We can draw from it a reasonable idea of the immensity of God's love but do not have the faculties to understand it fully. However, if we think often of these great mysteries and meditate often on the passion we will become students of the passion and gain a little more knowledge and insight with each passing day into the seriousness of sin, which we take so much for granted and the immensity of God's love for us, which we also take for granted.

Third, did we at least accomplish our goal of finding out just who killed The Christ? Yes! That we did do. Who do you think killed him? Let's examine each character or set of characters one at a time.

Was it Judas? Judas was ever at the side of Christ when he thought he had something to gain from it. He desired power and wealth and for a time he thought that Our Lord would become king over Israel giving him the prestige and money he desired. When he finally realized that this was not Our Lord's mission and that he was falling from grace with the real powers to be, he turned on him hoping to gain favor with those who could really grant him wealth and power. While he did not kill him he made it possible with his betrayal. He thought more of satisfying his avarice than Our Lord's innocence and was a big part of the conspiracy.

Was it Annas, the former High Priest? Annas was the moving force behind almost every plot that we read about in the Gospel accounts to ensnare Our Lord. He is the one who held all the back door meetings with Judas to seal the deal for the Apostle to betray his Master. He tried his level best to convict him of blasphemy in the first illegal religious trial but failed miserably. Although he was one of the major forces in the conspiracy against Christ and certainly wanted him dead, he did not kill him.

The next major players in this sad conspiracy are Joseph Ciaphas and the Sanhedrin. Ciaphas was the reigning High Priest of the day and the Sanhedrin was the ruling council over all civil and religious affairs in Israel. They in effect ran the nation by not only enacting rules and laws but by enforcing and judging them also. Ciaphas made no attempt to hide his hatred for Our Lord who was upsetting the status quo and exposing their wrong doings. He kind of succeeded where Annas had failed in that he got a finding of blasphemy by getting Our Lord to tell the truth about himself which he could not accept. They sentenced him to death but had no authority to carry out the sentence which only Roman authorities could render. Although they would have killed him if they could have, they did not, but figure very heavily in the conspiracy to do so.

We are not having much luck here, are we? We have lots of players but no winners so far. Now enter Pontius Pilate, the Roman Governor and Legion commander. In reality he doesn't want to be bothered and doesn't even want to hear their charges. He finally listens to their accusations and finding out that he is a Galilean sends him off the Herod and believes he is done with the affair.

Herod sees the whole affair as a magic act and when Our Lord refuses to work a miracle for him he judges him to be a fool has him badly treated and sends him back to Pilate. He refuses to sentence him to death and actually takes no part in the conspiracy to kill him.

Even though Pilate has him back he still wants no part of the whole affair. He tries many ways to release him even to the point of practically killing him with whips. When push comes to shove and he believes that the Jewish leaders will make him look bad to Caesar he knowingly condemns Our Lord to death while believing him to be innocent to preserve his own skin. So we got our man, right? Wrong. Yes he did sentence him to death although in his own twisted mind he exonerated himself. He put all the wheels into motion that would lead to his death but he did not kill him.

So what about the Jewish people? Didn't they demand his death? "Let his blood be on us and upon our Children." They certainly added to the madness of the day but they had a great deal of faith in their leaders who almost enjoyed celebrity status and they were easily led astray. By the end of the day many repented of their actions and some even converted including Pharisees, Priests and people. While the Jewish people in and around the Praetorium that day cannot fully exonerate themselves from the conspiracy, the only worry they gave Pilate was the possibility of insurrection. Pilate's condemnation was influenced by the Jewish leaders and the possibility of insurrection. The Jewish people did not kill him.

What about us then? What about the many sins of the entire human race from the time of Adam until the time of the last person to walk the face of the earth? What about all our collective sins and our lack of concern for goodness and holiness? Did we as the human race collectively cause the death of Christ? Our sins certainly laid the ground work for it to happen. Because of our sins it was necessary that a God-Man suffer and die to atone for these affronts to the Almighty and for us to be redeemed. If we were to enjoy salvation and share in the Heavenly Kingdom it was necessary that the Christ should die. However, we collectively as the human race did not kill him.

Was it the Roman soldiers then? Sorry, soldiers did not normally perform the lowly acts of execution. These particular soldiers began the day with complete indifference. They were carrying out their orders which were to maintain order. They gave no thought to who was being crucified or why. They did not volunteer to be there, they were assigned to this detail. They did not take any hands on part in the crucifixion. Before it was over, many were converted and provided a military escort for their new king's burial service. They were not even part of the conspiracy.

Then it had to be those dregs of humanity, those pagan executioners who with seemingly great glee and brutality carried out the crucifixion; finally killing him. They certainly tried to kill him and they honestly thought they were killing him. It is almost certain that when all was said and done if you had asked them if they had killed him they would have answered yes. They would be wrong! Although they did everything necessary to bring about his death as they were obviously well trained to do, they did not kill him.

Okay, if it was none of the above then it had to be the Centurion Cassius Gaius with his spear. Sorry! He was already dead, so the thrust of the lance could not have had any effect other than to bring forth the blood and water.

So now that we have eliminated all the players; who killed the Christ? The correct answer is that no one killed him. He came into the world to die in atonement for all the sins of mankind but he did not come to be killed. He came as a sacrifice.

Many times during the passion following the normal course of events Our Lord should have died. No matter how hard they tried, and try hard they did, they were not able to kill him. They tried many times out of fear that Pilate would release him.

When Our Lord was nailed to his cross the cross became an Altar. He himself was the sacrifice which was firmly fixed upon the Altar and raised aloft for all to see. A sacrifice can't be offered by just anyone, it must be offered by a Priest. If a lamb is killed by just anyone is just a dead lamb. If a lamb is killed by a Priest as an offering to God it is a sacrifice. He is the Lamb of God. If he had been killed by just anyone there would just have been a death and not a sacrifice. His death had to be brought about by a Priest of the proper order. He, being the Lamb of God is Priest and sacrifice and therefore must bring about his own death. For this purpose he came into the world.

When his hour had come, he freely exercised his own will and gave up his life in atonement to God for the redemption of the human race. A supreme act of love for all mankind and for each and everyone of us individually.

If you had been the only one to respond to his redemptive act he would have still done it, exactly the same horrendous way, just for you! Think about it!!

Recommended Reading

Holy Scripture
Old and New Testament

City of God – By Mary of Agreda
World Apostolate of Fatima
Blue Army Shrine
P.O. Box 976
Washington, New Jersey 07882
Four Volumes
These are wonderful volumes full of in depth reading into the life of Christ as dictated by the Blessed Virgin to Ven. Mary of Agreda. A must not only for all Catholic homes but all Christians homes as well.

The Dolorous Passion of Our Lord Jesus Christ
By Ven. Anne Catherine Emmerich
Tan Books and Publishers
P.O. Box 410487
Charlotte, NC 07882
Also a must for any serious student of the Passion

The Watches of the Sacred Passion
By Fr. P. Gallwey, S.J.
Manresa Press, Roehampton, S.W.
Great Britain
Two Volumes
A masterful set of books written in the style of the spiritual exercises of St Ignatius of Loyola

The History of the Passion
By Fr. James Groenings, S.J.
B. Herder, St Louis, Mo.

Jerusalem – City of Jesus
By Fr Richard M. Mackowski, S.J
William B. Eerdmans Publishing Co.
Grand Rapids, Mi.

The Passion and Death of Jesus Christ
By St Alphonsus De Liguori
Mount St Alphonsus Book Shop
Esophus, N.Y.

A Doctor at Calvary
By Pierre Barbet, M.D.
Image books
A Division of Doubleday & Co, Inc.
Garden City, N.Y.

Revelations of St Bridget
Tan Books and Publishers
P.O. Box 410487
Charlotte, NC 28241

The Shroud of Turin
By Fr Vittorio Guerrera
Tan books and Publishers
P.O. Box 410487
Charlotte, NC 28241